KU-061-107

Contents

Introduction

Assessment in its different forms is an inescapable part of everyday life. We have all been subjected to assessment of the most obvious and formal kind when we have taken an examination, been interviewed for a job or taken a driving test. We are also engaged in the process of assessment whenever judgements are made about us (or when we evaluate other people) on the basis of, for example, appearance, speech and behaviour. However, the results of these assessments become more significant for us when the results have a direct effect on our lives, ie when they are 'high stakes'. This book is concerned with the testing of numeracy – one of the abilities that organizations, including employers and educational institutions, frequently assess for purposes of selection. For many people, selection tests present a serious obstacle to obtaining a place on a course, a job or, for those in employment, promotion to a more senior level. Many people fail to perform as well as they might on such tests because:

- they are over-anxious and nervous;
- they are out of practice with the techniques used when taking tests;

▓   they are unfamiliar with the ways in which test items or questions are posed and the methods by which they are expected to respond – problems that may be exacerbated if they are required to take a test online, as is increasingly likely;

▓   through reliance on electronic calculators they may have become unaccustomed to doing even the most simple arithmetic calculations either in their heads or on paper.

It is rare for candidates to be allowed to use calculators when taking selection tests. Consequently, your performance will be seriously impaired unless you have practised your basic number skills without the aid of a calculator, particularly under the time pressure you will be subjected to when taking a real test. Careful and systematic preparation for a selection test, including the use of the practice numeracy tests such as the ones provided here, can help you to overcome these common causes of failure. It will also help you to avoid the sense of frustration that comes from knowing that you have missed an opportunity because, when it mattered, you have not performed to the best of your ability.

The main purpose of this book, therefore, is to inform readers about selection tests in general and to offer guidance on how you might prepare yourself for taking them. However, a large proportion of its content consists of practice tests of the type known as 'numeracy' or 'numerical reasoning' tests. These are commonly used for selection purposes in order to establish how competent candidates are in their ability to work with numbers – a basic requirement for many courses and jobs. By working systematically through the tests you will become more familiar with the techniques required to complete them successfully. Doing this will help you to build up your numeracy skills so that you will feel more confident when taking an actual selection test. You will find the answers to the practice tests in Chapter 8.

The practice tests in this book are similar to numeracy tests used widely for selection purposes. They have arisen from a wide range of training and development work undertaken by the authors with major employers such as Civil Service departments and agencies and the police. Many of the practice tests have been piloted by real candidates taking recruitment tests for entrance to the police service and to the Civil Service. Evaluation of the results of these pilot studies has demonstrated convincingly that regular use of these practice tests can significantly improve a candidate's performance, particularly when resitting a test that he or she has previously failed. Experience also shows that doing well on a test is not only a matter of intelligence and aptitude, but also a matter of confidence and determination. If you lack confidence then you are unlikely to perform to the best of your ability on any test. Our evaluation studies have shown that regular use of practice tests helps to boost the candidates' confidence, and so enables them to cope more effectively with the nervousness and stress that everyone feels when taking an important assessment test or 'high stakes' examinations.

Use of the practice tests provided here, therefore, should help you to:

- become familiar with the different types of numerical reasoning tests that are commonly used for selection purposes;
- learn to work more effectively under the pressure of time experienced in real tests;
- improve your test techniques so that you do not lose marks through simple errors.

The continuous feedback you will receive as you work through the tests should help to boost your self-confidence. This in turn should help to reduce your anxiety, nervousness and any tendency to panic when confronted with real selection tests.

However, in order to succeed you will need to be well motivated, to take practice seriously and to work hard on any weaknesses that become apparent in your results.

If you experience serious difficulty in coping with the practice tests given in the later chapters of this book it does not mean that you are a failure, and that you will never be able to succeed. What the practice tests will have done is to help you identify a learning need that you must address before you can make further progress. It is better to identify this weakness through practice tests than through the results of a selection test. If you find yourself in this situation, you will probably need to build up your basic numeracy skills before you continue to work on the practice tests as part of your preparation for taking a selection test. Your local further education college or adult education centre may be able to help you overcome this difficulty. The likelihood is that they will have on offer a variety of courses in basic numeracy with flexible patterns of study and ways of working (including e-learning packages) to suit a wide variety of circumstances including your own. Failing that, ask someone whom you know to have good number skills to act as your personal coach or mentor and help you to overcome the weaknesses you have identified.

A brief guide to selection tests

The aim of this chapter is to provide you with a brief guide to selection tests. In so doing, we will explain why employers and other organizations use selection tests, deal with issues of fairness and equity in test construction and administration, give a brief account of how tests are marked and outline the different types of test you might be required to take as part of a selection process.

Why do employers and others use selection tests?

In a highly competitive labour market many employers find that they receive large numbers of applications for jobs whenever vacancies occur. Many educational institutions find themselves in a similar situation with regard to places on their courses. In these circumstances, it is essential that every effort be made to ensure that the right person is chosen for the job or course. Wrong selection decisions can lead to poor performance, low morale and high rates of staff turnover, all of which can prove to be very costly to an employer and stressful to an employee or student. As most selection tests can be taken in large groups or online, they provide employers with a cost-effective means of choosing the most suitable people from large numbers of applicants. Those who achieve the test pass mark can then proceed to the next stage in the selection process, which may well include an interview and/or assessments of performance in a variety of exercises. Applicants for entrance to the police service, for example, are now required to attend an assessment centre at which their performance is assessed by means of two psychometric tests (one to assess their number skills and the other their verbal logical reasoning), two written exercises, four role-play exercises and, as if all that was not enough, an interview as well.

What are selection tests?

Selection tests are specifically designed to measure how good people are at certain skills. The use of tests in personnel selection is based on the assumption that there are stable job-related individual differences between candidates, and that these differences can be measured with sufficient accuracy to be of use to employers in their selection and promotion procedures. Research shows that well-constructed psychometric tests predict job performance better than almost any other single selection measure. Appropriate tests produce more accurate results than other, more commonly used, selection measures such as interviews or references from other people. Tests give objective information about a candidate and have been shown generally to lead to better and fairer selection decisions.

What is the difference between fair and unfair selection decisions?

Fairness in selection implies that applicants are chosen on the basis of aptitudes and abilities that can be shown to be relevant to a particular job and directly related to job performance. If selection decisions are not based on measures appropriate to the job, or the selection methods used are unreliable, then the selection may be unfair. The result might be that the most suitable candidates are rejected and the less suitable recruited or promoted.

Over many years, the British government has introduced a number of measures intended to ensure greater equality of opportunity for all its citizens. The Sex Discrimination Act 1975, the Race Relations Act 1976 and, in Northern Ireland, the Fair Employment (Northern Ireland) Acts 1976 and 1988 identify two types of discrimination, direct and indirect. 'Direct discrimination' involves treating someone less favourably on the basis of his or her ethnic origin, gender, marital status or, in Northern Ireland, religion. 'Indirect discrimination', on the other hand, may often be unintended and can arise through the use of selection tests. It occurs, in this context, if an employer requires applicants to obtain a particular score on a selection test, with which one group, defined, for example, by gender or race, finds it difficult to comply. When a test has the effect of disproportionately excluding one gender, ethnic or racial group it is said to have an *adverse impact*. This is not unknown in test usage, and differences in performance between males and females have been shown to occur from a relatively early age and continue into later life. For example, girls, as a group, have been shown to have outperformed boys in 11+ examinations by which pupils were (and in some areas still are) selected for various forms of secondary schooling. Similarly, males, as a group, were shown to outperform females on certain elements of the Executive Officer Qualifying Test (EOQT), which was used for entry to the Executive Officer grade in the Civil Service up until 1993. The reasons for these differences are extremely complex and include such things as differences in maturation rates, socio-economic backgrounds, learning opportunities and cultural and social attitudes. In the past, test scores were weighted to take account of the adverse impact that was known to occur in these tests.

How is fairness achieved in test construction and administration?

There are two elements to test fairness – the tests themselves and the way in which the tests are used. Test constructors will make great efforts to ensure that tests are fair. Every selection test will be accompanied by a test manual in which the steps taken to ensure fairness will be described. These steps will generally include:

- trialling with representative groups, which include ethnic minorities;
- checking for material that may be less familiar to some groups;
- providing detailed and carefully worded instructions;
- providing practice questions to help candidates become familiar with the test content and show what is expected of them;
- ensuring that the test is free from obscure or ambiguous questions;
- making certain that the test provides a reliable measure of particular attributes that are relevant to the job;
- providing normative data against which candidates can be properly compared.

When taking a test, candidates will be provided with a set of questions or problems that have to be answered in standardized conditions. The precise directions for the administration of a particular test will have been laid down by the test constructors in order that the test user can duplicate the administrative conditions with different groups of candidates. This is done in order to ensure that no group will have been advantaged or disadvantaged in terms of receiving the test instructions or in the way in which the test has been conducted. Although there may be slight variations, it is likely that most administrative conditions will have the following features:

- Candidates will be seated comfortably, facing the administrator and reasonably spaced apart if there are a number of people taking the test at the same time.
- Care will be taken to ensure that concentration will not be disturbed by telephone calls or visitors.
- If the test is an observation-skills test based on video recordings, then the administrator will ensure that all candidates have an uninterrupted view of the screen.
- Candidates will be provided with all the materials necessary to complete the test, eg pencils, erasers, answer sheets and scrap paper.
- The test session will begin with a brief introduction by the administrator. The administrator will explain the purpose of the test and tell candidates how the test is to be conducted. Many candidates will, naturally, feel nervous, and the administrator will attempt to alleviate any undue anxieties in order that candidates perform at their best.
- If the test requires candidates to provide gender and ethnic origin information then the administrator should explain that this is required for monitoring purposes only and not for use in the assessment of test results.
- All instructions are carefully worded to ensure that candidates have all the information they need in order to

complete the test correctly. The test administrator may read these instructions to the candidates and they may also be written in the test booklet. If this is the case, you should follow them as they are being read by the test administrator. In some tests, candidates are left to read the instructions by themselves, and this reading time may be included in the test time or additional time allocated for this purpose.

If time limits have been specified by the test constructor, these will be strictly observed. This is essential in order to ensure that no group gains an advantage over another, and as a consequence comparisons can be made between the performance of groups who take the test at different times.

Many tests provide example questions. In some tests, candidates are asked to attempt these, while others have them already completed. One of the important features that the administrator will draw candidates' attention to will be the way in which answers are to be recorded. Many tests are in a multiple-choice format (A to E in the example given below), and candidates are required to record their answers by blocking out the appropriate small box or circle:

A	B	C	D	E
□	□	■	□	□

The purpose of the sample questions is to ensure that candidates have a full understanding of what is required of them. If you use a tick or a cross, instead of a blacked-out circle or square, your answer may be recorded as incorrect even if the right choice has been made.

Candidates will generally then be given a final opportunity to ask questions about any of the test procedures before the administrator states clearly that the test has started.

The administrative instructions of some tests may not allow the administrator to give a warning that the end of the time allowed for the test is approaching.

How are tests marked?

Marking is usually a straightforward, but very important, part of testing. Obviously, it is essential that it is carried out correctly. Many tests will be objectively marked by the use of answer keys, on overlays, which are placed over the candidates' answer sheets. Before this is done, the answer sheets will be checked for any irregularities. This could, for example, include the candidate blocking out more than one circle or box where only one was required. If this happens, the marker will cross through the answer in such a way as to ensure that it is marked 'wrong'.

Optical mark readers are used for the machine scoring of certain types of answer sheets. Machine scoring is generally considered to give more reliable results than hand scoring and considerably increases the speed at which tests can be marked. This is very useful when large numbers of answer sheets have to be processed quickly.

If answer sheets are to be machine-scored it is particularly important that the test instructions are followed precisely. All circles or squares must be adequately filled in according to the instructions provided or the optical marker will not detect them. In such an instance the item will be marked 'wrong'.

What types of selection test might you be required to take?

A wide variety of tests is available to employers for selection purposes. The types that are most commonly used, together with the skills that they test, are described below.

Logical reasoning

Tests of this type are intended to establish your ability to solve problems by thinking logically on the basis of the information provided. These tests are intended to select people for jobs where in the day-to-day activities of the workplace you will be required to think critically and to solve problems as they arise.

Numerical reasoning

These tests are intended to determine your ability to handle numbers. You may be required, for example, to answer questions based on data presented in a variety of forms, including graphs and statistical tables. The level of difficulty of the problems will depend on the importance of numerical ability in the job to be undertaken. The tests are relevant to jobs where you will be required to work with numbers, such as handling money, dealing with numbers as part of work in science and technology, and interpreting numerical data in the form of diagrams of sales and production figures.

Verbal reasoning

These tests are intended to examine your ability to comprehend written information, and to understand and analyse the logic of written arguments. They are relevant to jobs where the understanding and evaluation of written information is an important skill. These are jobs where, for example, you might be required to read such things as reports and office circulars, memos from colleagues and letters from customers.

Error checking

These tests are intended to examine your ability to check the accuracy of information that may be presented in a variety of forms. They are relevant to jobs where you might be required, for example, to check invoices against orders, data entered into a computer, or tables and accounts.

Data interpretation

These tests are intended to examine your ability to interpret facts and figures presented in the form of statistical tables and diagrams. They are relevant to jobs in offices, shops, engineering and management where you might be required to make sense of information presented in these ways.

Technical fault finding

These tests are intended to examine your ability to solve technical problems such as difficulties in various types of circuit or with machines. They are relevant to occupations where you may be required to take a logical approach in order to find faults in technical systems. Electricians, car mechanics, electronic technicians and computer programmers are examples of jobs that require skills of this kind.

Spatial reasoning

These tests are intended to examine your ability to visualize objects or drawings when looked at from different directions. They are, for example, relevant to jobs in design, planning and engineering, where you might be required to 'read' a plan and imagine how an object will look once it is finished.

2

How to prepare for taking selection tests

The aim of this chapter is to help you to understand how practice can have a positive effect on your test results by helping you to perform to the best of your ability. In so doing, we will give you guidance on how to use the practice tests and interpret your scores, and offer you advice on the other things you can do to improve your number skills.

Can practice make a difference?

The value of practice to improve performance is well recognized in many areas. In the performing arts, for example, pianists, dancers and singers are continually practising in order to maintain and further develop their skills. The value of practice in sport is perhaps best illustrated by a story that involves one of the world's leading golfers. In one particular tournament his ball finished in a sand bunker alongside the green, making his next shot very difficult. Nevertheless, he played the ball out of the bunker to land a short distance from the hole. A spectator shouted, 'That was lucky', to which the golfer replied, 'Yes, it's funny, the more I practise the luckier I seem to get!'

The same is true of performance on selection tests. As we pointed out in the Introduction, many candidates underachieve in tests because they are over-anxious or do not know what to expect. The practice tests provided here are designed to help you to overcome both of these common causes of failure. The practice tests in the later chapters of this book will help you to become familiar with common examples of the type of tests known as 'numerical reasoning'. Regular practice will also give you the opportunity to work under conditions similar to those you will experience when taking real tests. In particular, you should become accustomed to working under the pressure of the strict time limits imposed in real test situations. Familiarity with the demands of the tests and working under simulated test conditions should help you to cope better with any nervousness you experience when taking tests that really matter. Strictly speaking, the old adage that 'practice makes perfect' may not apply to selection tests, but regular practice can make a difference – for the better – by helping you to improve your scores!

How to perform to the best of your ability on tests

Our experience over many years of preparing candidates for both selection tests and public examinations leads us to suggest that if you want to perform to the best of your ability on tests you should:

- make sure that you know what you have to do before you start – if you do not understand, ask the test administrator;
- read the instructions carefully before the test starts in order to make sure that you understand them – skim reading through them can cause you to overlook important details and make silly mistakes;

▨ assume that the instructions (and the worked examples) are not the same as they were the last time you took the test – they may well have been changed, so read them as carefully as you can;

▨ highlight or underline the 'command words' in the instructions, ie those words that tell you what you have to do;

▨ work as quickly and accurately as you can once the test begins – every unanswered question is a scoring opportunity missed;

▨ check frequently to make sure that the question you are answering matches the space you are filling in on the answer grid (as emphasized in Chapter 1);

▨ avoid spending too much time on questions you find difficult – leave them and go back to them later if you have time;

▨ enter your best reasoned choice if you are uncertain about an answer (but avoid simply guessing);

▨ go back and check all your answers if you have any spare time after you have answered all the questions;

▨ keep working as hard as you can throughout the test – the more correct answers you get the higher your overall score will be;

▨ concentrate your mind on the test itself and nothing else – you cannot afford to allow yourself to be distracted;

▨ be positive in your attitude – previous failures in tests and examinations should not be allowed to have a detrimental effect on your performance on this occasion; don't allow yourself to be 'beaten before you begin'!

How to use the practice tests

To get the best out of the practice tests you should read and act on the advice given below. This consists of three sets of checklists to guide you through the different stages, ie before you begin, during the practice test and after you have completed it.

Before you begin to do any of the tests you should make sure that:

- you have the following: a supply of sharpened pencils, an eraser and some paper for doing any rough work;
- you have a clock or watch with an alarm that you can set to make sure that you work within the time limit you have set yourself;
- you are in a quiet room where you will not be disturbed or distracted and that has an uncluttered desk or table at which you can work;
- you have decided in advance which test you are going to tackle, and review what you learned from the previous practice session;
- you have read the instructions carefully on how to complete the test, even though you may think that you are already familiar with them;
- you have worked through the example(s) provided so that you know exactly what to do before you start.

You should then be ready to set your timer and turn your attention to the chosen practice test.

During the practice test you should try to:

- work quickly and systematically through the items – above all, don't panic;
- if you get stuck at any point move on to the next question as quickly as you can – you can always come back to any unfinished items at the end if you have time;
- remember to check over your answers if you have any spare time at the end;
- stop working as soon as the time is up (and mark the point you have reached in the test if there are any items that you have not yet completed).

After the practice test you should:

- check your answers by referring to the answers given under the appropriate headings in Chapter 8;
- put a √ against each question that you answered correctly and a × next to each one you got wrong;
- add up the number of ticks to give you your score on the test as a whole;
- compare your score with those on previous tests of the same type to see what progress you are making;
- work through any items that you did not manage to complete in the test and check your answers;
- try to work out where you went wrong with any questions that you answered incorrectly by working through the explanations given alongside the answers in Chapter 8. These will provide you with only one method for calculating the correct answer; there may well be alternatives that are much quicker – see if you can work them out.

If possible, talk through how you arrived at your answers with someone who has also done the test. Discussion of this kind can help to reinforce your learning by:

- helping you to understand why you got the wrong answer to certain questions;
- giving you a better understanding of the questions to which you managed to get the right answers;
- suggesting alternative ways of arriving at the same answer to a question, including short cuts you could use that will save you time – time you can then use on other items.

Discussion of this kind can help you to reach an understanding of the principles that underlie the construction of the test. In other words, you can begin to get 'inside the mind' of the person who set the questions. Working collaboratively with someone else can also help to keep you motivated and provide you with encouragement and moral support if and when you need it.

What do your practice test scores mean?

Because they tend to be shorter than real tests and have not been taken under the same conditions, you should not read too much into your practice test scores. You will usually find that the real tests you sit are more exacting because they will be:

- longer than the examples provided in this book;
- administered formally in a standardized way (described in Chapter 1) by a person who has been trained in their use;
- more stressful than practice tests.

Nevertheless, your practice test scores should provide you with feedback on the following:

- how your performance on the same type of test (eg number sequences or data interpretation) varies from one practice test to another, and hence what progress you are making over time;
- how well you are doing on one type of test (eg number problems) compared to another (eg number sequences), and so what your strengths and weaknesses appear to be.

However, when trying to make sense of your practice test scores you should remember that:

- in real tests your score will be compared with the performance of a group of typical candidates to determine how well you have done;

▓ the pass mark can go up or down depending on how many applicants there are and the number of vacancies that are available at any one time;

▓ most tests are designed to ensure that very few candidates, if any, manage to get full marks;

▓ as a general rule, the typical score for the majority of candidates sitting real tests will be a little over a *half of the maximum* available, though this can vary from test to test.

How to make the best use of feedback from practice tests

More important than your total score on a practice test is how you achieved that overall mark. For example, you could begin this diagnosis by making a note of the answers to the questions given below:

▓ How many questions did you attempt within the given time limit and how many remained unanswered?

▓ How many of the questions that you completed did you answer correctly?

▓ Where in the test were most of your incorrect answers (eg at the end when you were working in a hurry, or at the beginning when you may have been nervous or had not settled down properly)?

The answers to these questions should give you some pointers as to how you might improve your scores in future tests by changing your behaviour. For example:

▓ if you got most of the questions right but left too many unanswered, you should try to work more quickly next time;

■ if you managed to answer all the questions but got a lot of them wrong, you should try to work more accurately, even though that might mean that you have to work more slowly.

Remember, the object of the exercise is to score as many correct answers as you can in the time allowed. Thus, there is a balance to be struck between speed and accuracy. Intelligent practice and careful evaluation of your results can help you to reach the right balance for you.

Other things you can do to improve your numeracy skills

Numeracy tests seek to measure how effectively you can function with numbers. The computations involved in solving the numeracy problems included in such tests have to be done quickly and accurately. In order to do this you must be able to **add, subtract, multiply** and **divide**. Obvious though this may seem, the increased use of electronic calculators in schools and in the workplace has resulted in large numbers of people lacking confidence in their ability to perform these basic arithmetical functions either in their heads or on paper.

One of the most useful mathematical 'aids' that will help you to improve your performance on numeracy tests is a knowledge of **multiplication tables**. This should enable you to multiply and divide numbers quickly and accurately without the help of a calculator. If you do not know your tables already then our advice to you would be: learn them. One way of doing this is to construct a 'multiplication matrix' using the outline grid provided in Table 2.1. Once completed, you can refer to it whenever you need to check that you have got the right answer to a simple multiplication or division problem. However, as far as we are concerned, this is one instance where rote learning, reinforced by practice, can be very effective. Once you have a working knowledge of your tables you will be able to save a lot of time when taking selection tests – and be able to work much more accurately.

Regular practice of your basic arithmetic skills will help to improve your performance when taking numeracy tests, and there are many opportunities in everyday life in which you can do this. For example, you can:

- calculate the cost of the contents of your shopping trolley before you reach the checkout;
- use the exchange-rate tables in a daily newspaper to work out how many units of foreign currencies you would receive for a given number of pounds sterling;
- use the tables given in the weather sections of a daily newspaper to calculate the difference in temperature between the world's warmest city and the world's coldest city, or the length of time between sunrise and sunset in London.

There are any number of basic numeracy problems that you could set yourself whenever you have an odd 5 or 10 minutes to spare. It is important, however, to ensure that you are able to provide yourself with feedback to check on the accuracy of your calculations. For this reason it might be helpful if you carry a pocket calculator with you in order to check whether your answers to the problems you set yourself are right or wrong.

Some suggestions for particular aspects of numeracy to work on are set out below in the form of a checklist. However, before you begin to put any of them into practice you should bear in mind the need to adopt a systematic approach to the development of your numeracy skills. You will not achieve the improvements you want to make by picking out areas at random from the checklist and trying them out spasmodically. Identify the areas in which you need to improve and then work consistently to a plan. Remember that regular practice and revision will help you to improve.

Basic numeracy checklist

Try to ensure that you are competent in the following aspects of numeracy, all of which occur frequently in selection tests:

- weights and measures;
- units of time;
- adding, subtracting, multiplying and dividing fractions;
- adding, subtracting, multiplying and dividing decimals;
- calculating the areas of shapes such as rectangles;
- calculating averages (eg speeds);
- calculating percentages;
- extracting numerical information from line graphs, bar graphs, pie charts and statistical tables and using it as the basis for making calculations.

Since metric and non-metric measuring systems are common in everyday use (eg weights, money, linear distances), numeracy tests used for selection purposes usually include both. Hence you need to make yourself familiar with them and competent in their use.

It should be remembered that the benefits you are seeking to gain are cumulative – small improvements building on each other incrementally. It is more likely that such gains will be achieved by consistent application over a period of time measured in weeks and months rather than by a last-ditch effort just before you take an important test. Preparing for tests and examinations is a bit like training for a race – it is the fitness that you build up over the long term that enables you to 'peak' at the right time.

Multiplication matrix

Take a look at the 'multiplication matrix' in Table 2.1. Once completed, this will give you the answer to any multiplication problem involving two numbers up to and including the number 12. A quick look at the matrix shows that 2 × 7 = 14; 3 × 3 = 9; and 4 × 12 = 48. Now complete the matrix and then use it to help you to commit your multiplication tables to memory. When you have done that, add additional numbers to the matrix and learn them in the same way.

Table 2.1   Multiplication matrix

1	2	3	4	5	6	7	8	9	10	11	12
2						14					
3		9							30		
4											48
5				25							
6										66	
7						49					
8											96
9			36					81			
10	20										
11				55							
12						96					

Taking real tests

The aim of this chapter is to offer you some guidance on what to do when taking real tests – before the event itself, during the test and after you have taken it. In particular, advice is given on the different ways you might be expected to record your answers in 'paper-and-pencil' versions of such tests. Finally, some pointers are given as to what to expect if you are asked to complete a numeracy test online, together with details of some websites you might visit in order to prepare yourself for such an experience.

What to do when taking real tests

Before taking any tests, for example as part of the selection process for a job or for training, you should:

- find out as much as you can about the test in advance, eg ask if any examples are available of the types of question you will be asked;
- try to get a good night's sleep before the test;
- make sure that you get to the place where the test is to be held in good time so that you do not get anxious through having to rush;

- ensure that you have your glasses, contact lenses or hearing aid available if you need to use them during the test;
- inform the organization or employer conducting the test in advance about any disability you may have so that they can make the necessary arrangements for you.

At the test itself you should:

- listen very carefully to the instructions you are given by the person administering the test;
- do exactly what you are told to do;
- read the written instructions very carefully – it could prove to be very costly if you fail to do so;
- work your way carefully step by step through any practice questions that may be provided – they are there to ensure that you know exactly what to do;
- make sure that you understand how you are required to record your answers;
- ask the test administrator if there is anything that you do not understand about the procedures – it's too late now to ask anything about the content of the test;
- when told to begin the test, read each question carefully before answering;
- work as quickly and accurately as you can;
- keep an eye on the time;
- stop working immediately when told to do so.

After the test you should:

- avoid worrying about your test results and get on with the rest of the selection process – people are usually selected by an employer for reasons other than high test scores;
- when it is appropriate to do so, ask for feedback on your performance even if you are not offered the job or a place

on the training scheme – it may help you to be successful the next time.

How to record your answers

In the practice tests provided here you will find that the questions and the answer spaces are presented together. However, when you take real tests you will generally find that separate question and answer sheets or booklets will be used. This is because electronic scanners or optical mark readers (see Chapter 1) are often used to mark and score the test papers, especially with large organizations such as Civil Service departments and agencies.

It is essential, therefore, that your answers are presented in a form that the machine can understand. The instructions at the start of the test will usually inform you exactly how to mark your answers, eg:

Boxes must be marked with a dark pencil mark that completely fills in the response position on the answer sheet. Light or partial marks □, ticks ☑ oblique strokes ▨ or crosses ☒ will be ignored and marked wrong.

Some questions will ask you to mark two or more circles/ boxes instead of one, so read the question carefully, as an incorrect number of responses will also be marked wrong. If you make a mistake or change your mind, erase all un-intentional marks completely from the answer grid with a rubber.

Many questions are presented in a multiple-choice format in which you are required to choose the correct answer from the given alternatives and to record this by putting a mark against the box or circle of your choice. For example, if you decide that the answer to a particular question is the one labelled B, you would record your answer like this:

A   O   B   ●   C   O   D   O

If boxes were being used instead of circles and you decide that the answer to a particular question is the one labelled 3, you would record your answer like this:

1   □   2   □   3   ■   4   □

Whichever system is used, you must take care to follow the instructions exactly – marks placed incorrectly will lead to your answer being marked wrong.

Taking tests online

Much of the advice given above assumes that the numeracy test you will be given will be hard copy and you will be expected to fill in your answers using some form of writing implement – a so-called 'paper-and-pencil' test. However, it is becoming more than likely that you will be asked to complete your tests 'online', ie sitting in front of a computer screen on which the test items appear and using a keyboard and mouse to record your answers. If that is the case, there is nothing to worry about in doing electronic versions of numeracy tests. The number skills they are seeking to assess will be the same – all that will be different is the mode of presentation and the methods by which you are expected to respond. In both cases these will not be dissimilar to those with which you are familiar – though it should be noted that the technology allows for different kinds of response, such as 'picking and placing' lines in their correct position on a graph or objects on a diagram. However, you will still need to:

- read the on-screen instructions carefully (and any you have been given on paper in advance);
- follow the instructions you have been given, especially those that inform you about how much time you have available and how you are expected to record your answers.

If you already have the keyboard skills needed to cope with the demands of such a test, you might even find it to be more fun than doing one by paper and pencil – many in your situation do.

Given the medium in which we are writing, it has been impossible to give you examples here, but why not go to the web to complete a practice test or two? Given below are a few places to look at for a start – you should be able to find others:

- Morrisby Organisation Tests: www.morrisby.co.uk
- Saville & Holdsworth: www.shldirect.com
- Tests from Team Technology: www.teamtechnology.co.uk
- Civil Service: www.selfassess.faststream.gov.uk
- Move on: www.move-on.org.uk
- www.keyskills4u.com

Number problem tests

This is a multiple-choice test, the aim of which is to test your basic numeracy skills. To that end, you will be presented with a series of number problems for which you are required to choose the correct answers from a choice of five possible answers (A–E). You do not have to show how you arrived at your answers – you simply indicate your choice in each case according to the instructions. You are not allowed to use a calculator in tests of this kind, so you should try to work without one whenever you can. This applies particularly when you are attempting to work out the answers to the number problems in the examples and the practice tests given below. However, you can use a calculator at the end to check your answers – especially if you happen to have run into difficulties.

Sample questions

The sample questions given below should help to give you an idea of what is involved before you start work on the practice tests. It is suggested that you work your way through them, writing your answers in the boxes provided. The answers are given in Table 4.1.

Q1.   How much would it cost to buy eight packets of frozen peas at 92p a packet?

A	B	C	D	E
£6.96	£7.16	£7.36	£7.46	£7.66

Answer =

Q2.   If I pay £12.54 for wood and £1.49 for screws, how much will I have spent in total?

A	B	C	D	E
£13.93	£14.03	£14.13	£14.93	£15.03

Answer =

Q3.   When full, a multi-storey car park can hold 540 cars. How many empty spaces are there when the car park is only half-full?

A	B	C	D	E
1,080	280	54	270	370

Answer =

Q4.   Your taxi ride to the station takes 28 minutes and your train journey then takes 45 minutes (including any waiting time). How long does your journey take in total?

A	B	C	D	E
63 min	70 min	73 min	83 min	85 min

Answer =

Q5. Out of 23,850 people in a cricket ground, 30% had bought tickets in advance. How many people paid to get in on the day?

A	B	C	D	E
1,695	7,155	10,695	16,665	16,695

Answer =

Q6. Each pack contains enough laminate to cover 4 sq metres. How many packs would you need to buy to cover an area of flooring that measures 40 metres by 40 metres?

A	B	C	D	E
400	20	220	40	440

Answer =

Q7. The aim of a residents' survey is to sample 1 out of every 9 households. If there were 117 households in a street, how many would be included in the sample?

A	B	C	D	E
10	11	12	13	14

Answer =

Q8.   Four streets have the following number of houses in them: 36; 48; 91; and 127. What is the average number of houses per street?

A   B   C   D   E
69.50   70.50   72.50   73.50   75.50

Answer =

Q9.   A motorist is caught on a radar camera travelling at 57.8 mph in an area where the speed limit is 40 mph. By how much was the driver exceeding the speed limit?

A   B   C   D   E
17.2 mph   17.8 mph   18.2 mph   18.8 mph   27.8 mph

Answer =

Q10. How many 5-litre cans of liquid would be needed to fill a 150-litre storage tank?

A   B   C   D   E
20   25   30   35   40

Answer =

If you look closely at the number problems given in the above sample questions you will see that they are aimed at assessing your ability to use the four basic rules of arithmetic:

Addition

Subtraction

Multiplication

Division

In so doing, you are required to show that you are able to work in:

Whole numbers

Fractions

Decimals

Averages

Percentages

Ratios (and proportions)

Finally, you have to be able to use the basic rules of arithmetic skills and different types of numbers in the calculation of:

Money

Numbers of objects

Speed

Time

Area

Volume

Table 4.1 shows how these principles have been applied in the sample questions given above, together with the answers. In each case, one method for calculating the answer is given in brackets. There may be quicker alternative methods or short cuts – try to work them out for yourself.

Reviewing your basic numeracy skills

Before moving on to the practice tests, you should consider whether or not you need to revise your basic number skills. You can start this process by making use of the checklists given above. For each of the number skills in the lists, all you have to do is to decide how competent you think you are and record your decision in the appropriate box by writing a number, where:

- 1 = I am good at this;
- 2 = I can do this most of the time, but with some difficulty under pressure;
- 3 = I need to work on this to reach the required standard.

Having done this, you should try to do some remedial work on any of the number skills that fall into category 2 or category 3. You can do this by working your way through the relevant sections of *How to Pass Numerical Reasoning Tests: A step-by-step guide to learning the basic skills* by Heidi Smith, published

Table 4.1   Sample questions: answers and principles

Question	Answer	Basic rules of arithmetic	Types of number	Application of number
1	**C** (92p × 8 = £7.36)	Multiplication	Decimals	Money
2	**B** (£12.54 + £1.49 = £14.03)	Addition	Decimals	Money
3	**D** (540 ÷ 2 = 270)	Division	Fractions	Objects (cars)
4	**C** (28 + 45 = 73)	Addition	Whole numbers	Time
5	**E** (100% − 30% = 70%; 10% of 23,850 = 2,385 × 7 = 70% = 16,695)	Subtractions Division Multiplication	Whole numbers Percentages	Objects (people)
6	**A** (40 × 40 = 1,600 ÷ 4 = 400)	Multiplication Division	Whole numbers	Area
7	**D** (117 ÷ 9 = 13)	Division	Whole numbers Ratios	Objects (households)
8	**E** (36 + 48 + 91 + 127 = 302 ÷ 4 = 75.50)	Addition Division	Averages Decimals	Objects (houses)
9	**B** (57.8 − 40.0 = 17.8)	Subtraction	Decimals	Speed
10	**C** (150 ÷ 5 = 30)	Division	Whole numbers	Liquids

by Kogan Page. Building on your strengths and addressing your weaknesses (should you have any) will have the advantage of improving your chances of doing well in the practice tests. In turn, this should boost your confidence when the time comes to take the real test.

Number problem practice tests

Once you feel ready to do so, move on to the number problem practice tests given below. Each test consists of **25 questions** for which you should allow yourself **12 minutes** per test. Work as quickly and as accurately as you can. Use a sheet of paper or a notepad for any rough work. If you are not sure of an answer, mark your best choice, but avoid wild guessing. If you want to change an answer, rub it out completely and then write your new answer in the space provided. If you want to put pressure on yourself, reduce the amount of time you allow yourself to complete the test as a whole – allowing yourself **10 minutes** instead of 12 minutes will have the effect of making the test more difficult because you will have less time per item to work out the correct answer and to check at the end to see if you have made any mistakes.

The answers are given on pages 166–74 together with a brief explanation as to how they have been calculated. Remember that in most cases there may well be alternative methods for arriving at the correct answer including short cuts – try to work these out for yourself and, when you have done that, decide which ones work best for you. Give yourself one mark for each question you get right, and make a note of the scores to see if you are improving from one test to another.

After each test, you should take some time to work your way through it item by item, making sure that you understand how to arrive at the correct answer. You should also check to see if there is a pattern to any errors you happen to be making – you might have a weakness, which will cost you marks unless you do something about it.

Test 1

Q1.   Two out of every eight cyclists are questioned in a spot-check. Out of 408 cyclists, how many are questioned?

A	B	C	D	E
102	100	88	80	40

Answer =

Q2.   If I pay £4.40 for lunch and £2.75 for tea, how much in total have I spent?

A	B	C	D	E
£6.95	£7.05	£7.15	£7.25	£7.35

Answer =

Q3.   A worker's shift begins at 05.30 and lasts for 9 hours. What time does it end?

A	B	C	D	E
15.30	15.00	14.30	14.00	13.30

Answer =

Q4. How much would it cost to buy 3 bicycle lights at £3.50 each?

A	B	C	D	E
£9.50	£11.50	£12.00	£11.00	£10.50

Answer =

Q5. If I pay 23p for a bus ticket, £2.35 for a train ticket and £10.40 for a taxi fare, how much have I spent in total?

A	B	C	D	E
£2.98	£5.75	£9.98	£10.63	£12.98

Answer =

Q6. If my bus journey takes 35 minutes and my train journey takes 55 minutes, how long is my journey in total?

A	B	C	D	E
1½ hours	1¼ hours	70 minutes	¾ hour	85 minutes

Answer =

Q7. I leave my house at 06.00 and return at 14.15. How many hours have I been out of my house?

A	B	C	D	E
20½	18¾	8¼	6	2¼

Answer =

Q8. If 5 lorries fill up their tanks with 120 litres of diesel
     each, how many litres of diesel are used in total?

A   B   C   D   E
6,000   600   500   460   240

Answer =

Q9. A car park holds 550 cars when it is full. How many cars
     does it hold when it is half-full?

A   B   C   D   E
1,100   250   55   275   350

Answer =

Q10. In a car park of 660 cars, 20 per cent of the cars are
     yellow. How many yellow cars are there in the car park?

A   B   C   D   E
680   230   330   132   33

Answer =

Q11. If a machinist earns £110 a week, how much will she
     earn in 12 weeks?

A   B   C   D   E
£12,000   £1,210   £1,320   £1,120   £122

Answer =

Q12. A motorist is travelling at 72.5 mph in an area where the speed limit is 50 mph. By how much is the driver exceeding the speed limit?

A	B	C	D	E
20.5 mph	22.5 mph	52.5 mph	70.5 mph	120.5 mph

Answer =

Q13. If a police officer is asked for directions on average 3 times a day, how many times will she be asked for directions in a 7-day period?

A	B	C	D	E
4	10	17	21	27

Answer =

Q14. Out of 13,750 people in a football stadium, 10 per cent are season ticket holders. How many people do not have a season ticket?

A	B	C	D	E
1,375	1,775	10,750	12,375	15,125

Answer =

Q15. If I ran 18 miles in 3 hours, what is my average speed?

A	B	C	D	E
21 mph	13 mph	8 mph	6 mph	3 mph

Answer =

Q16. My shift is 9 hours long. If I begin work at 13.30, what time do I finish work?

A	B	C	D	E
04.30	09.30	19.30	21.00	22.30

Answer =

Q17. Each roll of wallpaper is 1 metre wide. How many vertical widths of wallpaper are needed to paper a wall that is 12,500 cm long?

A	B	C	D	E
12,500	125	25	12.5	2.5

Answer =

Q18. One pack contains enough tiles to cover an area that measures 2 metres × 2 metres. How many packs of tiles are needed to cover a floor 40 metres × 40 metres?

A	B	C	D	E
440	400	200	40	20

Answer =

Q19. How much would it cost to buy 7 envelopes at 23p each?

A	B	C	D	E
73p	£1.41	£1.61	£1.81	£2.10

Answer =

Q20. A crate of milk contains 8 bottles and costs £4.00. How much do 3 bottles of milk cost?

A	B	C	D	E
£2.40	£1.48	£1.24	£1.50	£2.50

Answer =

Q21. A survey showed that 1/8 adult males over the age of 65 years owned a mobile phone. What is this fraction as a percentage?

A	B	C	D	E
8%	9%	10.5%	12.5%	17.5%

Answer =

Q22. Whilst on a foreign holiday a tourist changes £125 into kroner. The exchange rate is 12 kroner for £1. How many kroner does the tourist receive?

A	B	C	D	E
1,250	1,375	1,500	1,625	1,750

Answer =

Q23. A person fills up her car with 40 litres of diesel. She wants to know how many gallons she has bought and uses the conversion 4.5 litres = 1 gallon. How many gallons of diesel (correct to two decimal places) did she buy?

A
4.50

B
8.88

C
9.48

D
12.50

E
18.00

Answer =

Q24. There are 105 calories in an ounce of cheese. If 1 ounce = 30 grams, how many calories are there in 300 grams of cheese?

A
615

B
705

C
945

D
1,050

E
1,125

Answer =

Q25. The distance between point A and point B is 97 miles. 1 mile is the equivalent of 1.6 kilometres. What is the distance between point A and point B to the nearest kilometre?

A
155 km

B
162 km

C
165 km

D
170 km

E
175 km

Answer =

Test 2

Q1. I began the day with £10.00 in my pocket. By the evening I had £2.73 left. How much had I spent?

A	B	C	D	E
£10.73	£8.73	£7.27	£6.27	£2.73

Answer =

Q2. My shift starts at 06.30 and ends at 14.30. How many hours will I have worked if I work for 7 days?

A	B	C	D	E
56	48	46	38	36

Answer =

Q3. I earn £110 per week. I am given a 5 per cent pay rise. What will my new weekly wage be?

A	B	C	D	E
£125.00	£115.50	£115.00	£110.50	£105.00

Answer =

Q4. What percentage of £32.00 is £8.00?

A	B	C	D	E
8%	20%	23%	25%	32%

Answer =

Q5.   If two pairs of boots cost £46.00, how much would one
      pair cost?

A   B   C   D   E
£10.50   £11.50   £13.00   £23.00   £26.00

Answer =

Q6.   The police station is 1,180 metres from the library. The
      supermarket is halfway between the police station and
      the library. How many metres is the supermarket from
      the library?

A   B   C   D   E
2,360   1,200   590   600   1,800

Answer =

Q7.   If I drive at 30 mph, how long (in hours) will it take me
      to drive 90 miles?

A   B   C   D   E
½   3   6   9   12

Answer =

Q8. How many square metres of turf will I need to cover two areas of ground, one of which is 7 metres × 3 metres and the other 4.5 metres × 2.5 metres?

A	B	C	D	E
31.5	31.75	32	32.25	32.5

Answer =

Q9. If I drive 200 miles, how many hours will the journey take if I drive 40 mph for 100 miles and 80 mph for 100 miles?

A	B	C	D	E
3¾	4¾	5	3½	3

Answer =

Q10. If 9 out of 10 cars use unleaded petrol, what percentage of cars use leaded petrol?

A	B	C	D	E
90%	80%	81%	10%	9%

Answer =

Q11. If the house subsides at a rate of 2 cm per year, how many years will it be before it has subsided half a metre?

A	B	C	D	E
500	50	25	12½	½

Answer =

Q12. The blue car costs £3,500, the red car costs £6,700 and the green car costs £7,800. What is the average price of these 3 cars?

A	B	C	D	E
£18,000	£12,500	£9,000	£6,000	£3,000

Answer =

Q13. A book of stamps used to cost £2.00. Now it costs £2.40. By what percentage has the price increased?

A	B	C	D	E
120%	100%	20%	12%	5%

Answer =

Q14. Bob is 29 years old, Peter is 27 years old and Sally is 33 years old. What is the total (in years) of all their ages?

A	B	C	D	E
79	83	89	90	97

Answer =

Q15. If you walk along a straight stretch of road from the post office past the hospital to the bus station, how far will you have walked in metres if the post office is 120 metres from the hospital, and the hospital is 189 metres from the bus station?

A	B	C	D	E
389	309	299	189	69

Answer =

Q16. A bus carrying 26 passengers arrives 8 minutes late at the factory. How many minutes of work is lost in total by the 26 passengers?

A	B	C	D	E
340	308	268	208	8

Answer =

Q17. Each lorry holds 220 litres of petrol. How many lorries will a 2,420-litre tank fill?

A	B	C	D	E
10	11	12	22	100

Answer =

Q18. What percentage of £8.00 is 20p?

A	B	C	D	E
16%	10%	8%	2.5%	2%

Answer =

Q19. There are 75 police officers at a football match. If one-third of the officers are inside the ground and the rest are outside, how many are outside the ground?

A	B	C	D	E
100	50	33	25	12

Answer =

Q20. A person works for two-thirds of a 24-hour day. How many hours does the person work in 5 days?

A	B	C	D	E
120	96	80	48	24

Answer =

Q21. On a map, the distance between point A and point B measures 7.6 cm. The scale of the map is 1 cm : 20 km. What is the actual distance between point A and point B to the nearest kilometre?

A	B	C	D	E
126 km	132 km	145 km	149 km	152 km

Answer =

Q22. To change from Celsius (C) to Fahrenheit (F), use the following rule: multiply the degrees Celsius by 9, divide by 5, then add 32. If the temperature at noon one day was 26.5C, what was the temperature in Fahrenheit?

A	B	C	D	E
77.9	79.7	81.6	83.4	89.7

Answer =

Q23. A builder charges £110 for concreting 5 sq m plus a fixed charge of £35. The area to be concreted is a rectangle 2.5 m wide by 3 m long. How much will the builder charge?

A	B	C	D	E
£110	£135	£165	£200	£210

Answer =

Q24. A man takes a taxi to collect the food from a takeaway. The fare is £3.60 each way and he makes this up to £4 each way to include a tip. The food costs £24.40 and he also buys 10 cans of drink at 96p per can. The man and his three friends share the costs equally between them. How much does each of them pay?

A	B	C	D	E
£9.50	£10.00	£10.50	£11.20	£11.50

Answer =

Q25. A man is planning to paint one side of his garden fence. One tin of paint covers 5 sq m and the instructions state that to be effective 2 coats must be applied. The fence is 7.5 m long and 2.0 m high. How many tins of paint will he have to buy?

A	B	C	D	E
3	4	5	6	7

Answer =

Test 3

Q1. If 1 litre of paint covers an area of 60 metres by 10 metres, how many litres of paint are needed to cover a wall 30 metres by 5 metres?

A	B	C	D	E
6	2	0.5	0.25	0.33

Answer =

Q2. If I have £7.37 in my pocket, and spend £3.43 and have £1.52 left in my pocket, how much money must I have lost?

A	B	C	D	E
£12.32	£4.95	£3.94	£2.42	£1.52

Answer =

Q3. How many complete lengths of rope, each 4.7 metres long, can be cut from a rope 92 metres long?

A	B	C	D	E
21	20	19	16	11

Answer =

Q4. If someone earning £140 a week receives a pay increase of 2.5 per cent, by how much will the pay increase?

A	B	C	D	E
£2.00	£2.50	£3.00	£3.50	£4.00

Answer =

Q5. If it takes me 20 minutes to water a garden that is 25 square metres, how many minutes will it take me to water a garden that is 50 metres × 2.5 metres?

A	B	C	D	E
120	100	80	60	40

Answer =

Q6. On 4 consecutive days I work the following hours: 06.00 to 14.00; 07.30 to 18.00; 07.00 to 13.00; and 08.30 to 19.30. How many hours am I not working over those 4 days?

A	B	C	D	E
96	60½	60	38½	35½

Answer =

Q7. What is the average height of 5 people whose heights are 2.01 m, 1.92 m, 1.57 m, 1.88 m and 2.05 m?

A
188.6 cm

B
180 cm

C
18.9 cm

D
1.89 cm

E
1.88 cm

Answer =

Q8. If prices rise by 8 per cent, what would be the new price of an item now costing £160.00?

A
£172.80

B
£170.00

C
£168.00

D
£166.00

E
£162.80

Answer =

Q9. How many 7 cm × 7 cm tiles are needed to cover a surface that measures 84 cm × 84 cm?

A
164

B
144

C
124

D
120

E
84

Answer =

Q10. The speed limit in an area is 40 mph. If I were travelling at 67.5 mph, by how much would I have to reduce my speed so that I was travelling at the speed limit?

A
40 mph

B
33.5 mph

C
30 mph

D
27.5 mph

E
23.5 mph

Answer =

Q11. If I paid 5 parking fines of £12.00 each, how much have I paid in total?

A	B	C	D	E
£62.00	£60.00	£52.00	£50.00	£48.00

Answer =

Q12. Seven 57-seat buses are booked to carry a football supporters' club to a match. How many supporters can travel on the buses?

A	B	C	D	E
399	449	499	549	599

Answer =

Q13. The money from four safes, each containing £352.00, has been stolen. How much money in total has been stolen?

A	B	C	D	E
£1,652.00	£1,408.00	£1,208.00	£1,052.00	£888.00

Answer =

Q14. It takes me 7 hours to travel 420 miles. What is my average speed?

A	B	C	D	E
70 mph	62 mph	60 mph	40 mph	35 mph

Answer =

Q15. If a shopper has £37.00 and spends £21.32, how much change will she have?

A	B	C	D	E
£19.32	£18.58	£17.68	£16.58	£15.68

Answer =

Q16. A survey samples 1 out of every 9 households. Out of 117 households, how many will be sampled?

A	B	C	D	E
10	11	12	13	14

Answer =

Q17. The average weekly wage is £213.00. If I earn only one-third of this, how much do I earn?

A	B	C	D	E
£71.00	£69.00	£142.00	£141.00	£73.00

Answer =

Q18. The number of arrests has risen by 6 per cent this year. What is the total number of arrests this year, if 500 arrests were made last year?

A	B	C	D	E
800	630	530	506	30

Answer =

Q19. If I work 18 out of 24 hours, what percentage of the day have I worked?

A	B	C	D	E
25	35	50	65	75

Answer =

Q20. A person spends 40 per cent of his weekly wage on clothes. He earns £230.00 a week. In 2 weeks, how much has he spent on clothes?

A	B	C	D	E
£92	£102	£115	£164	£184

Answer =

Q21. A club has a membership of 2,498 of whom 1,004 are women. What is the closest estimate of the ratio of men to women members?

A	B	C	D	E
7 to 5	3 to 2	5 to 2	9 to 4	12 to 5

Answer =

Q22. A survey by the staff at a fitness centre showed that 5 out of 8 of the male users worked out in the gym at least three times a week. What percentage of male users work out in the gym at least three times per week?

A	B	C	D	E
26.5%	40.5%	52.5%	62.5%	72.60%

Answer =

Q23. A company has a total workforce of 600 employees. Their weekly wages are as follows: 184 less than £200; 294 £200–£399; 92 £400–£599; and 30 £600 or more. Approximately what percentage of the workforce earn £400 or more per week?

A	B	C	D	E
35%	25%	20%	15%	10%

Answer =

Q24. The sketch given below shows the shape and dimensions of a kitchen floor, which the owner intends to tile. What is the area of the floor?

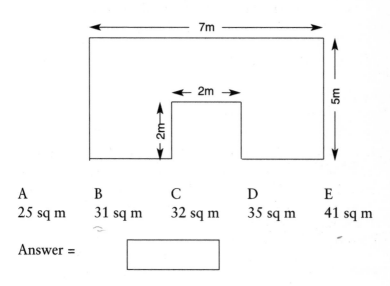

A	B	C	D	E
25 sq m	31 sq m	32 sq m	35 sq m	41 sq m

Answer =

Q25. A householder's quarterly electricity bill is made up of a fixed charge of £15.75, plus 8.4 pence for every unit used. What would the total bill be if the householder had used 783 units of electricity?

A	B	C	D	E
£65.77	£74.40	£81.52	£85.50	£91.57

Answer =

Test 4

Q1.   A roll of wire is 100 metres long. How many rolls are needed to surround a square park that measures 500 metres × 500 metres?

A	B	C	D	E
2,500	200	20	10	5

Answer =

Q2.   My garden is 13 metres square, of which half is paved. How many square metres are unpaved?

A	B	C	D	E
169	139	84.5	42.25	6.5

Answer =

Q3.   Four streets have the following number of houses on them: 18; 23; 41; 37. What is the average number of houses per street?

A	B	C	D	E
29.75	31.75	33	37.5	119

Answer =

Q4.   The ages of a group of people are: 29; 47; 53; 17; 48; 59; 22; and 33. What percentage are over 40 years of age?

A	B	C	D	E
60%	50%	40%	10%	4%

Answer =

Q5.   I had £12.43 and spent £7.67. How much did I have left?

A	B	C	D	E
£5.67	£5.03	£4.83	£4.76	£3.64

Answer =

Q6.   I was caught speeding in a 50 mph area. I was travelling 23 mph above the speed limit. How fast was I travelling?

A	B	C	D	E
83 mph	73 mph	67 mph	63 mph	27 mph

Answer =

Q7.   Six people share the £14.46 taxi fare, each person adding 50p as a tip for the driver. How much does it cost each person?

A	B	C	D	E
£4.12	£3.61	£2.81	£2.61	£2.91

Answer =

Q8.   How many 15-litre drums are needed to fill up a 450-litre tank, which already contains 90 litres?

A	B	C	D	E
30	24	20	15	13

Answer =

Q9.   A survey showed that there was an average of 5 accidents an hour. How many accidents would you expect to occur in one full day?

A	B	C	D	E
96	112	120	125	150

Answer =

Q10.   A worker's shift begins at 04.30 and ends at 13.15. How many hours does that person work in a 5-day working week?

A	B	C	D	E
43¾	42¼	43	44¾	47¼

Answer =

Q11. What is the average speed of 5 cars travelling at the following speeds: 60 mph, 75 mph, 25 mph, 40 mph, 50 mph?

A	B	C	D	E
45 mph	50 mph	55 mph	60 mph	65 mph

Answer =

Q12. 75 per cent of the spectators in a stadium that holds 1,244 people are under cover. When the stadium is full, how many spectators are not under cover?

A	B	C	D	E
1,033	933	811	411	311

Answer =

Q13. How many hours will it take a cyclist to travel 67.5 miles at an average speed of 9 mph?

A	B	C	D	E
5½	6½	7	7½	8

Answer =

Q14. A shopper spends £29.99 on shoes, £23.50 on trousers and £18.00 on a shirt. How much will he have left if he started with £120?

A	B	C	D	E
£61.49	£58.51	£51.49	£48.51	£41.49

Answer =

Q15. A shop reduces all of its prices by 12.5 per cent. What is the sale price of a chair that originally cost £160?

A	B	C	D	E
£145	£140	£135	£130	£125

Answer =

Q16. A garage charges £45 for parts and £105 for labour. How much is the total bill when VAT charged at 17.5 per cent is added?

A	B	C	D	E
£156.25	£166.25	£176.25	£186.25	£196.25

Answer =

Q17. How many fencing panels would be needed to enclose a garden that is 24 metres long and 9 metres wide if the panels are 3 metres long by 2 metres high?

A	B	C	D	E
11	22	26	48	72

Answer =

Q18. A betting syndicate of five people wins £140. What was the total profit if they each staked £2.50?

A	B	C	D	E
£137.50	£135.00	£132.50	£130.00	£127.50

Answer =

Q19. In one week a person worked 35 hours at normal time
and 6 hours' overtime at double the rate for normal time.
How much did the person earn if the normal time rate of
pay was £6.00 an hour?

A	B	C	D	E
£252	£262	£272	£282	£292

Answer =

Q20. How many miles will a lorry have travelled if it main-
tained an average speed of 35 mph for 6½ hours?

A	B	C	D	E
220	222.5	225	227.5	230

Answer =

Q21. A customer buys four items of clothing that cost £35,
£45, £55 and £250 including VAT charged at 17.5%. If
the overall cost was reduced by a discount of 15% per
item, what would be the customer's final bill?

A	B	C	D	E
£297.75	£327.25	£337.50	£347.25	£352.25

Answer =

Q22. In 2000, a company employed 350 men and 150 women. By 2005 the overall size of the company's workforce remained the same but it now employed 275 men and 225 women. As a percentage of the total workforce, by how much did the number of women employees increase between 2000 and 2005?

A   B   C   D   E
10%   12.5%   15%   17.5%   20%

Answer =

Q23. A survey of the travelling times (in minutes) from home to school of a group of 10 students produced the following results:

25   25   30   30   50   20   15   10   20   35

What was the average journey time to school in minutes?

A   B   C   D   E
23.50   24.00   25.25   26.00   27.50

Answer =

Q24. A builder is making a path using slabs of concrete that are 80 cm long, 20 cm wide and 2.5 cm thick. What is the volume of a single slab of concrete in cubic centimetres?

A   B   C   D   E
250   1,000   1,750   2,500   4,000

Answer =

Q25. A customer withdraws £425 from her bank account. She gets £25 in £5 notes, half of the remaining sum in £20 notes and the rest in £10 notes. How many notes does she receive?

A	B	C	D	E
40	35	30	25	20

Answer =

Data interpretation tests (1)

The data interpretation tests provided in this chapter are similar to the multiple-choice tests commonly used in personnel selection. Typically, a test of this type consists of a series of statistical tables followed by a set of questions related to each table. For each question, there are five possible answers – though in some tests this may be reduced to four. Your task is to work out which is the correct answer to each question from the options you are given, and to record your choice in the space provided. In order to do this, you have to use the data presented in the relevant table. This is illustrated in the sample question given below.

Price of fuel for heating in pence per useful kilowatt hour:

Fuel	Pence
Butane (room heater)	4.6
Electricity (fan heater)	5.2
Kerosene (central heating)	2.9
Gas (wall heater)	1.7
Coal (open fire)	3.5
Anthracite (central heating)	2.2

Q1.   Which heating fuel is approximately twice the price of gas?

Butane   Electricity   Kerosene   Coal   Anthracite

Answer = | Coal |

Although these questions may look very different from the number problems that we dealt with in Chapter 4, the data interpretation questions you will meet in this chapter and Chapter 6 do in fact have many similarities. For example, they are still aimed at assessing your ability to use the four basic rules of arithmetic, ie addition, subtraction, multiplication and division. You are also required to show that you can work competently in whole numbers, fractions, decimals, averages, percentages, ratios and proportions. Finally, you will still have to use your skills in these basic rules of arithmetic and different types of numbers in order to perform calculations in contexts in which they are applied to such units as money, speed, time, area, volume, rainfall and temperature.

Data interpretation practice tests

Four practice tests are provided for you to work through, each consisting of **20 questions**. You should allow yourself **25 minutes** to complete each test. Your aim should be to work as quickly and as accurately as you can, attempting as many questions as possible in the time allowed. Again, if you wish to put pressure on yourself you can try to complete the tests in less time than that suggested above. The answers are given on pages 174–83. One method for calculating the answer is given in each case, but remember that there may well be quicker alternatives or short cuts – so try to work them out for yourself if you can.

Test 1

The following table shows the number of emergencies attended by six fire brigade sub-stations during a five-month period:

Sub-station	May	June	July	Aug	Sept
A	11	10	12	26	27
B	22	23	20	42	28
C	36	46	58	68	43
D	21	22	24	27	26
E	16	16	15	19	12
F	24	18	26	37	29

Q1. What was the total number of emergencies attended by all six sub-stations in June and July?

283   309   290   310   287

Answer =

Q2. Which of the following sub-stations had the biggest increase in the number of emergencies attended in August compared to July?

A   B   C   D   E

Answer =

Q3.   If sub-station C had attended only half the number of
      emergencies over the five-month period, which of the
      following sub-stations would have attended most emer-
      gencies?

A   B   C   D   E

Answer =

Q4.   What percentage of the total number of emergencies in
      September were attended by sub-station C?

23%   24%   25%   26%   27%

Answer =

Polls of the voting intentions of a sample of the population
were carried out over a period of six months and the
percentage support for the different political parties was as
follows:

Month	Party A	Party B	Party C	Party D	Party E
Jan	18	20	24	17	21
Feb	18	22	22	18	20
Mar	19	23	21	20	17
Apr	22	23	21	21	13
May	23	24	18	20	15
June	24	25	18	17	16

Q5. In which month was there the greatest difference
     between the party gaining the most support and the
     party gaining the least support?

January   February   March   April   May

Answer =

Q6   Which two parties received the same level of support
     over the six-month period?

A and B   D and E   C and E   A and C   B and D

Answer =

Q7. If Party A received only half of the support given to it in
     June and instead the support was distributed among
     Parties C, D and E, with Party E benefiting by twice as
     much as each of the other two, which two parties would
     have received the greatest amount of support in the
     month of June?

B and C   D and E   C and E   B and D   B and E

Answer =

Q8. If the sample was made up of 5,000 people, how many
     indicated in June that they would vote for party D?

800   825   850   900   950

Answer =

Five shops averaged the following monthly sales of sports goods in one calendar year:

Items	A	B	Shops C	D	E
Footballs	30	14	24	30	20
Shorts	29	24	24	34	32
Shirts	20	30	32	34	16
Boots	30	44	40	22	18
Trainers	40	22	36	21	26
Tracksuits	20	24	24	28	14

Q9. Which two shops sold the same total number of items?

A and B   C and D   B and C   D and E   A and D

Answer =

Q10. If each sales assistant in shop C sold 24 items, with the exception of one who sold 36 items, how many sales assistants are there in shop C?

6   7   8   9   10

Answer =

Q11. If the staff of shop C had sold only half the number of items they did, and shops A and D had sold no track-suits, which shop would have sold the most items?

A   B   C   D   E

Answer =

Q12. If the average sales price of the trainers sold in shop B was £57.50, what was the total amount taken in shop B from the sale of trainers?

£1,165   £1,265   £1,365   £1,465   £1,565

Answer =

The sources of income of five British universities in one year were as follows:

Source	University				
	A	B	C	D	E
	%	%	%	%	%
Public funds	48	46	54	46	58
Research contracts	21	16	20	19	16
Investments	16	10	12	19	10
Conferences	8	14	9	6	5
Vacation lettings	4	8	3	7	6
Donations	3	6	2	3	5

Q13. Which two universities received the same proportion of their income from combined public funds and research contracts sources?

A and B   C and D   B and C   D and E   C and E

Answer =

Q14. Which university received the greatest proportion of its total income from research contracts, investments and vacation lettings combined?

A   B   C   D   E

Answer =

Q15. Which university received the smallest proportion of its total income from investments and donations combined?

A   B   C   D   E

Answer =

Q16. If the total income of university D was £28.7 million, how much was received from vacation lettings?

£1,700,000 £1,920,000 £2,009,000 £2,090,000 £2,170,000

Answer =

The percentage unemployment rates in five countries, over a five-year period, were as follows:

Country	2000	2001	2002	2003	2004
A	4.2	4.6	4.9	5.3	5.5
B	4.4	4.5	4.4	4.3	4.6
C	4.9	5.1	5.3	5.6	5.0
D	8.7	9.0	9.2	9.4	9.0
E	5.4	5.9	5.9	6.3	6.8
F	6.8	7.0	7.2	7.5	8.1

Q17. In which two countries was there the same percentage increase in unemployment in 2004 compared to 2000?

A and B   A and F   B and C   D and E   B and E

Answer =

Q18. What was the average percentage change in unemployment across all six countries in 2004 compared to 2003?

−0.2   −0.1   +0.1   +0.2   +0.3

Answer =

Q19. What was the difference in the unemployment rate, averaged over the five-year period, in country D compared to country E?

1   2   3   4   5

Answer =

Q20. If the population of country D has been comparatively stable at about 65 million over the five-year period, approximately how many more people were unemployed in 2004 compared with 2000?

1,950   19,500   195,000   1,950,000   19,500,000

Answer =

Test 2

The percentage of households owning durable items in five regions were:

| | | | Region | | |
Item	A	B	C	D	E
Microwave	48	41	49	46	43
Fridge	63	61	69	60	64
Dishwasher	11	7	11	10	8
Washing machine	82	85	87	83	80
Freezer	41	33	45	42	44
Tumble dryer	32	33	27	28	26

Q1. Which region had the highest percentage of households not owning a microwave?

A   B   C   D   E

Answer =

Q2. If a further 4 per cent of households in each of regions A and B owned dishwashers, together with a further 5 per cent in region C, what would be the average percentage of households owning dishwashers across all five regions?

9   10   11   12   13

Answer =

Q3.   What was the average percentage of households without a washing machine?

14.6   15.6   16.6   17.6   18.6

Answer =

Selected crime statistics in the first quarter of one year in five divisions of one police force are shown in the following table:

Incidents	Divisions				
	A	**B**	**C**	**D**	**E**
Robbery	68	99	52	52	62
Wounding	26	27	14	29	24
Theft	30	84	31	27	29
Arson	31	38	30	30	26
Indecent assault	17	12	15	21	18
Fraud	156	90	101	160	115

Q4.   If the incidents of fraud are omitted, which two divisions have the same number of reported criminal incidents?

A and B   C and D   B and C   D and E   B and E

Answer =

Q5. If the criminal statistics for the second quarter of the year
     show a 6 per cent increase, what would be the total
     number of criminal incidents in Division B for the half-
     year?

700   707   718   721   730

Answer =   [   ]

Q6. If about 92% of the robberies resulted in successful pros-
     ecutions, how many convictions for robbery were there?

300   302   304   306   308

Answer =   [   ]

The classes in a local primary school managed to raise the
following amounts during a school year:

			Class		
Event	A	B	C	D	E
Raffle	£32	£14	£24	£30	£20
Jumble sale	£20	£24	£24	£34	£32
Car boot sale	£10	£30	£32	£34	£16
Concert	£30	£44	£40	£14	£18
Sponsored walk	£62	£8	£18	£42	£22
Sports day	£8	£24	£24	£28	£14

Q7.   Which two classes raised the same amount as each other?

A and B   C and E   B and D   A and C   B and E

Answer =

Q8.   If each pupil in Class C raised £9 overall, with the exception of Tracey, who raised £18, how many pupils are there in Class C?

15   16   17   18   19

Answer =

Q9.   If Class A had raised only half the amount that they did for each event, and Class B had not taken part in the concert, which event would have raised the most money when funds from all classes were combined?

| 15 | 16 | 17 | 18 | 19 |
| Raffle | Jumble sale | Car boot sale | Concert | Sponsored walk |

Answer =

Q10. What percentage of the money raised by Class E was through the jumble sale?

14%   20%   26%   32%   38%

Answer =

Trends in the relative market value of selected groups of commodities are given below:

Commodity	2000	2001	Year 2002	2003	2004
Beverages	95	92	86	72	76
Cereals	75	68	62	66	60
Fats and oils	76	70	68	62	58
Timber	82	76	100	98	96
Metals	80	62	64	84	88
Minerals	79	74	72	66	73

Q11. What is the average difference in the relative value of the six commodities in 2004 compared to 2000?

+8   +4   –5   –6   +36

Answer =

Q12. Which value showed the greatest amount of change in 2004 compared to 2000?

Beverages   Cereals   Fats and oils   Timber   Metals

Answer =

Q13. Which commodity showed the least variation in value over the period from 2000 to 2004?

Beverages   Cereals   Fats and oils   Timber   Minerals

Answer =

Monthly repayments (in £) on a loan for different periods are shown in the following table:

		Years		
Loan	10	15	20	25
1,000	12.50	10.50	9.00	8.50
2,000	25.00	20.50	18.00	16.00
10,000	129.50	103.00	90.00	84.50
15,000	194.00	154.50	135.00	126.50
20,000	259.00	206.00	180.00	168.00

Q14. How much more would be repaid on a loan of £20,000 taken out over 20 years compared to the same loan taken out over a period of 15 years?

£3,000   £4,250   £5,250   £6,120   £7,200

Answer =

Q15. What is the total amount repaid over 25 years of a loan of £15,000?

£22,300   £37,950   £45,300   £55,800   £66,100

Answer =

Q16. The monthly repayment on a loan of £15,000 over 20 years is reduced to £125.00. By how much will this reduce the total amount repaid on the loan over the full period?

£1,200   £2,400   £3,100   £3,900   £4,800

Answer =

The percentage increase in the annual retail prices of selected items in one store during the period 1999–2004 is shown in the following table:

Item	Price in 1999	% increase on 1999 price				
		2000	2001	2002	2003	2004
Washing machine	£340	2.4	4.6	5.8	7.6	8.8
Dryer	£200	2.0	5.4	7.1	8.8	10.6
Dishwasher	£240	2.8	4.6	6.4	7.9	9.8
Vacuum cleaner	£125	2.7	4.8	6.3	7.7	9.3
Stereo unit	£120	1.5	3.5	5.2	7.5	9.8
TV	£265	2.0	4.5	6.2	7.9	9.5

Q17. How much more would a washing machine and dryer cost in 2004 compared to 1999?

£21.12   £31.12   £41.12   £51.12   £61.12

Answer =

Q18. In which two years was the combined annual percentage increase in the price of the six items the same?

1999/2000 2000/2001 2001/2002 2002/2003 2003/2004

Answer =

Q19. In the 2004 January sales, one shop reduced the price of televisions by 25%. How much will the sale price be?

£198.75   £216.74   £217.64   £242.54   £271.84

Answer =

Q20. What was the difference in the cost of a vacuum cleaner in 2003 compared to 2001?

£1.63   £2.63   £3.63   £4.63   £5.63

Answer =

Test 3

A set of examination results showed that the percentages of candidates gaining pass grades in the A to E range in selected subjects were as follows:

			Grade		
Subject	A	B	C	D	E
Biology	11.9	15.0	15.5	17.1	15.7
Chemistry	16.1	17.6	15.0	15.0	13.6
Computing	8.0	12.5	17.0	19.0	19.5
English	9.9	17.9	20.9	20.8	15.7
Geography	10.5	14.2	17.9	19.8	16.2
Mathematics	17.2	14.5	14.1	14.3	13.4

Q1. What percentage of candidates failed to achieve a pass grade (A–E) in Chemistry?

20.7   21.7   22.7   23.7   24.7

Answer =

Q2. In which subject did the greatest percentage of candidates gain a pass grade (A–E)?

Biology   Chemistry   Computing   English   Geography

Answer =

Q3. If 46,540 candidates sat Biology and 42,440 candidates sat Geography, what was the difference (to the nearest 100) in the number of candidates who obtained an A grade in these two subjects?

800   900   1,000   1,100   1,200

Answer =

Q4. A total of 28,860 candidates sat the computing examination. How many failed to obtain a grade?

5,926   6,226   6,526   6,926   7,226

Answer =

The world prices of the main agricultural commodities (US$ per tonne) for a five-year period were:

			Year		
Commodity	1	2	3	4	5
Beef	205	150	155	160	165
Wheat	178	136	112	135	140
Butter	124	84	75	90	98
Maize	120	75	68	80	82
Sugar	10	15	27	42	45
Milk powder	70	65	88	120	138

Q5.   In which two years would the total cost of buying 1 tonne of each of the six commodities have been the same?

1 and 2   1 and 3   2 and 4   4 and 5   2 and 3

Answer =

Q6.   Which two commodities showed the same change in price in Year 5 compared to Year 1?

Beef   Maize   Beef   Wheat   Wheat
and sugar   and sugar   and wheat   and maize   and sugar

Answer =

Q7.   If prices had risen by 5 per cent per tonne during Year 5 for all commodities except beef, which decreased by 12 per cent per tonne, what would the approximate difference in the overall cost of buying 1 tonne of each of the six commodities in Year 6 have been compared to Year 1?

−8   −5   +2   +5   +8

Answer =

The Safe Travel Insurance Company issued the following table of premiums for holiday insurance:

	Premiums per person		
	Area A	Area B	Area C
Period of travel	(UK)	(Europe)	(Worldwide)
1–4 days	£8.50	£12.50	£16.00
5–8 days	£10.50	£15.00	£18.00
9–17 days	£12.50	£16.00	£24.50
18–23 days	£15.50	£22.00	£36.00
24–31 days	£20.50	£30.50	£44.50
32–62 days	£38.50	£49.00	£62.00

Winter sports: cover at 3 times these premiums.
Discount for children: 20% reduction for each child under 14.

Q8.   What would be the total premium paid by 2 adults and 2 children (both over 14) holidaying in the UK from 7 August to 17 August?

£42   £48   £50   £52   £60

Answer =

Q9.   What would be the total premium paid by 3 adults having a winter sports holiday in Europe from 7 to 14 January?

£45   £95   £115   £135   £145

Answer =

Q10. What would be the cost of insuring a party of 2 adults and 2 children (aged 15 and 12) on a 14-day skiing holiday in the United States?

£98   £192.60   £279.30   £294   £312.60

Answer =

Q11. If the insurance premiums are increased by 15 per cent, what would be the new combined premium for a party of 4 adults taking a 21-day holiday in Spain?

£91.20   £101.20   £110.20   £111.20   £121.20

Answer =

The percentage increase in prices over a five-year period is shown in the following table:

| Item | Average family weekly spending 1999 Year 1 | % increase on Year 1 spending | | | | |
		2000 Year 2	2001 Year 3	2002 Year 4	2003 Year 5	2004 Year 6
Food	£50	2.3	4.8	7.8	11.6	15.6
Alcohol	£19	0.3	2.3	7.9	17.1	21.7
Housing	£46	3.3	8.4	14.0	20.5	28.5
Fuel/light	£18	1.3	6.0	9.9	14.5	20.9
Transport	£25	0.5	0.5	2.1	6.7	9.9
Clothing	£22	2.0	3.5	4.9	7.0	9.9
Other	£34	0.2	1.8	3.4	7.2	11.0
Total	£214					

Q12. If an average family bought the same food in Year 6 as they had in Year 1, how much would their weekly food bill have cost in Year 6?

£57.80   £58.20   £62.20   £67.80   £72.20

Answer =

Q13. If the Green family bought 15 per cent more clothing and 5 per cent less food than the average family, by approximately how much would their weekly bill have differed from that of the average family in Year 1?

+£1.80   +£0.80   –£0.20   –£0.80   –£1.80

Answer =

Q14. If the average family weekly spending had increased by 25% in Year 6, how much (to the nearest pound) would the average family have left to spend after paying for housing, fuel and light?

£181   £183   £185   £187   £190

Answer =

Q15. Which item showed the biggest percentage increase from Year 3 to Year 6?

Food   Alcohol   Housing   Fuel/light   Transport

Answer =

The local scout troops have managed to raise the following amounts for charity:

Event	Red	Blue	Troop Green	Yellow	Brown
Jumble sale	£20	£12	£17	£20	£15
Raffle	£15	£17	£17	£22	£21
Car cleaning	£15	£17	£21	£22	£13
Gardening	£20	£27	£25	£12	£14
Summer fête	£36	£9	£14	£26	£16
Sponsored hike	£5	£17	£17	£19	£12

Q16. Which two troops raised the same amount as each other?

Red and blue	Yellow and Green	Brown and Red	Brown and Blue	Red ✓ and Green

Answer =

Q17. If each scout in Green Troop raised £14 overall, with the exception of Leroy, who raised £27, how many scouts are there in Green Troop?

6   7   8   9   10

Answer =

Q18. If Red Troop had raised only half the amount that they did for each event, and Blue Troop had not done any gardening, which event would have raised the most money?

Raffle   Gardening Car   Jumble   Summer
                         cleaning   sale   fête

Answer =   .   [   ]

Q19. The aim of the fundraising is to buy a wheelchair costing £386. How much money will remain after paying for the wheelchair to donate to another charity?

£117   £127   £137   £147   £157

Answer =   [   ]

Q20. If on the next occasion Brown Troop succeeded in increasing the amount it raised for charity by 20%, how much would it raise in total?

£100.10   £105.15   £107.25   £109.20   £118.30

Answer =   [   ]

Test 4

A guide to personal loan repayments is given in the following table:

Monthly repayments for loans taken out over periods of 1 to 5 years

Amount of loan	1	2	3	4	5
£1,000	£89.67	£48.00	£34.11	£27.17	£23.00
£5,000	£448.00	£240.00	£170.56	£135.80	£115.00
£10,000	£887.50	£487.50	£331.94	£262.50	£220.83
£20,000	£1,775.00	£975.00	£663.88	£525.00	£441.67

Q1. How much interest (to the nearest pound) would be paid on a loan of £10,000 taken out over 3 years?

£1,940　　　£1,945　　　£1,950　　　£1,955　　　£1,960

Answer =

Q2. Mr Green takes out a loan of £5,000 over a 4-year period. How much (to the nearest pound) would remain to be paid after 3 years' repayments have been made?

£1,627　　　£1,628　　　£1,629　　　£1,630　　　£1,631

Answer =

Q3.   Mrs Brown took out and repaid a loan of £10,000 over
a 5-year period. How much would she have saved if she
had taken out and repaid the same loan over a 3-year
period?

£1,000   £1,100   £1,200   £1,300   £1,400

Answer =

Q4.   How much interest is paid on a loan of £20,000 taken
out over a 5-year period?

£6,000   £6,500   £7,000   £7,500   £8,000

Answer =

The bargain holiday prices of one tour operator in pounds per
person are:

	Number of nights					
	Period 1		Period 2		Period 3	
Hotel	7	14	7	14	7	14
A	231	374	235	380	200	320
B	174	260	178	291	140	210
C	156	226	162	223	120	181
D	150	218	156	222	145	178
E	148	210	154	218	145	175

Q5. Mr and Mrs Blue reserved a 14-night holiday for themselves at Hotel B in Period 2 and a 7-night holiday at the same hotel for their son and his partner during the same period. What was the combined cost of the holiday?

£712   £794   £874   £938   £1,164

Answer =

Q6. What would be the difference in cost of 4 people taking a 14-night holiday during Period 3 in Hotel A compared to the same period in Hotel E?

£480   £520   £540   £580   £600

Answer =

Q7. The holiday prices are increased by 8% for Period 1 and by 12 per cent for Period 2. How much more (to the nearest pound) would a holiday for 3 people staying at Hotel D for 14 nights in Period 2 cost, compared to 2 people staying in the same hotel for 14 nights in the same period, following the price rises?

£219   £229   £239   £249   £259

Answer =

Q8.   Following the price rises, what will the cost of a 14-night
      holiday be for 2 people in Hotel C with 7 nights in
      Period 1 and 7 nights in Period 2?

£680   £690   £700   £710   £720

Answer =   [   ]

The prices (per kilo) of selected food items in five supermarkets
were:

| | Supermarket | | | | |
| | A | B | C | D | E |
Food item	£	£	£	£	£
Beef	8.90	7.80	8.10	8.50	8.48
Cheese	5.80	5.60	4.95	5.40	5.25
Butter	4.60	4.85	4.82	4.10	4.36
Tomatoes	1.10	1.52	1.60	1.30	1.70
Potatoes	1.06	0.86	0.80	0.76	1.00
Apples	2.20	2.02	1.85	2.60	2.35

Q9.   If you were to buy 1 kilo of each of the food items, in
      which of the five supermarkets would the total cost be
      the least?

A   B   C   D   E

Answer =   [   ]

Q10. Which food item shows the greatest range in price (ie the difference between the cheapest and the most expensive) per kilo between the five supermarkets?

Beef   Cheese   Butter   Tomatoes   Bananas

Answer =

Q11. If supermarket A increases the price per kilo of beef by 5% and reduces the price per kilo of butter by 10%, what will be the approximate difference in the cost of 2 kilos of beef and 2 kilos of butter bought in supermarket A and the same items bought in supermarket C?

£1.07   £1.09   £1.11   £1.13   £1.15

Answer =

Q12. If a shopper bought the cheapest item from each of the supermarkets, what would the total cost of a shopping basket be if it contained 1 kilo of each food item?

£20.56   £20.66   £20.76   £20.86   £20.96

Answer =

The increase in the number of new cars sold by six main dealers in a six-year period was:

Dealer	Sales in 2000	Increase on sales in 2000				
		2001	2002	2003	2004	2005
A	846	10	17	26	60	66
B	928	13	19	26	41	53
C	690	13	16	19	24	37
D	760	11	18	25	32	39
E	866	10	15	31	37	46
F	584	12	21	33	40	57
Total	4,674					

Q13. What was the combined total number of cars sold by dealers A and D in 2005?

1,671   1,681   1,691   1,701   1,711

Answer =

Q14. What was the average number of car sales per dealer in 2003 (to the nearest 25)?

725   750   775   800   825

Answer =

Q15. If, in comparison with sales in 2000, the number of cars sold by dealer E in 2005 had increased by 8 per cent and the number of cars sold by the other dealers had increased by 10 per cent, what would the approximate increase have been in the combined number of cars sold by the dealers?

440   450   460   470   480

Answer =

Q16. Which dealer showed the greatest percentage increase in its annual sales in 2005 compared to those in 2000?

B   C   D   E   F

Answer =

The number of accidents attended by six emergency ambulance stations during a five-month period was:

Station	May	June	July	Aug	Sept
A	21	20	22	36	37
B	32	33	30	52	38
C	36	36	38	48	33
D	31	32	34	37	36
E	26	26	25	29	22
F	34	38	36	47	36

Q17. What was the percentage increase (rounded to the nearest whole number) in the number of emergencies attended during September compared to May?

8%   10%   12%   14%   16%

Answer =   [   ]

Q18. What was the approximate average increase in the number of emergencies attended by all six stations in August compared to July?

9   11   13   15   17

Answer =   [   ]

Q19. If, based on the figures for September, the statistics for the month of October show that the number of emergencies attended by Stations D and F have increased by 25 per cent, and the number attended by Station B decreased by 16 per cent, what would be the difference in the total number of emergencies attended by these three stations in October compared to September?

−6   +6   +12   +18   +24

Answer =   [   ]

Q20. Which two stations attended the same total number of emergencies over the five-month period?

A and C   D and F   B and C   C and F   B and F

Answer =   [   ]

Data interpretation tests (2)

The data interpretation tests provided here are similar to those given in Chapter 5, ie they are multiple-choice and they are commonly used in personnel selection. However, in this chapter, the numerical data upon which the questions are based are given a variety of forms, including graphs as well as statistical tables, though the style and format of the questions remain the same.

Numerical data are frequently presented diagrammatically in a variety of media, including newspapers, magazines and television. This is because showing information in this way enables patterns and relationships within a set of statistics to be displayed in a visual form, which can be more readily seen and supposedly understood. It is for this reason that tables, graphs and statistical diagrams also feature in the materials (hard copy or electronic) that many people are required to use at work or for the purposes of their education or training. It is not surprising, therefore, that they feature in the numeracy tests used in the process of selecting people.

You will know from Chapter 5 that in this type of test you are given a set of statistical data, which is then followed by five multiple-choice questions. Your task is to work out which is the correct answer to each question using the data provided, which on this occasion can be in the form of a graph or statistical diagram. As before, you simply record your answer in the spaces provided – there is no need to show how you arrived at your answers. As before, they are still aimed at assessing your ability to use the four basic rules of arithmetic and to show that you are competent in whole numbers, fractions, decimals, averages, percentages, proportions and ratios. Finally, you will still be expected to apply these skills to real-world contexts (past and present), such as those you might encounter in a newspaper, magazine, textbook or report, or on TV.

Before you tackle the practice tests, here are some guidelines that should help you to avoid making some common mistakes:

- Study the data carefully before you start answering the questions, including the heading, which not only tells you what the table, graph or diagram is about but often contains vital bits of information.
- Make sure that you understand how the information is arranged so that when you are asked to do so you will be able to extract the right piece of data, eg the *annual* (not *monthly*) sales figure for *Shop A* as opposed to *Shop B*.
- Study the scales of the graphs, which should be given up the side(s) of the graph (the so-called 'vertical axis') and along the bottom (the 'horizontal axis') – you may have to use them in order to extract the information you need to answer a question.
- Read the annotation on a graph or diagram very carefully – if you don't, it can mean that despite reading the right figure off a scale you have still given the wrong answer.
- Study the keys that are sometimes used with graphs and diagrams to show what the different forms of shading and lines mean – if you don't, you are likely to find yourself extracting the wrong piece of information needed to answer a question correctly.

Review the above list after you have completed each practice test and checked your answers. Try to revise it in the light of your experience.

Data interpretation practice tests

Four practice tests are provided below, each consisting of **20 questions**. Your aim should be to be able to complete such a test in **25 minutes**. However, as before, you might want to put additional pressure on yourself as you progress by reducing the amount of time you allow yourself. Try to work as quickly and as accurately as possible and to answer as many of the questions as you can in the time available. The answers, together with brief explanations as to how they have been arrived at, are given on pages 183–93.

Test 1

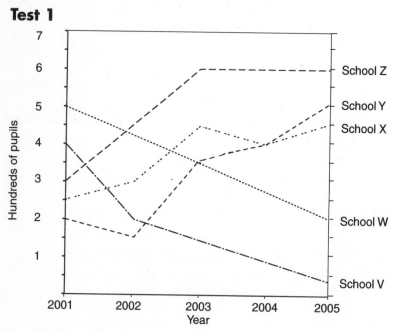

Figure 6.1 The number (in hundreds) of pupils at five rural schools from 2001 to 2005

Q1.   Which school had the most pupils in 2001?

V   W   X   Y   Z

Answer =

Q2.   What was the total number (in hundreds) of pupils at
      these five schools in 2003?

14   16   19   20   1,900

Answer =

Q3.   Which school showed a decrease in its pupil population
      at a constant rate from 2001 to 2005?

V   W   X   Y   Z

Answer =

Q4.   Which school had the same number of pupils in three
      consecutive years?

V   W   X   Y   Z

Answer =

Q5.   Which school increased its pupil population in each of
      the years between 2002 and 2005?

V   W   X   Y   Z

Answer =

The number of televisions (TVs), DVD players (DVDs) and radios (Rs) sold by five shops in April and September 2005:

| Shop | April | | | September | | |
	TVs	DVDs	Rs	TVs	DVDs	Rs
V	20	14	0	90	120	96
W	16	12	2	70	104	68
X	12	14	0	64	110	66
Y	20	16	0	104	150	86
Z	16	24	0	92	160	92

Q6. In September 2005, which shop sold the same number of televisions as it sold radios?

V   W   X   Y   Z

Answer =

Q7. In April 2005, one shop had the least difference in its sales of televisions and DVDs. Which shop was it?

V   W   X   Y   Z

Answer =

Q8. The number of DVDs sold by one shop in September 2005 was 6 times its sales of televisions in April 2005. Which shop was it?

V   W   X   Y   Z

Answer =

Q9. Which shop had the greatest increase in the actual number of DVDs sold in September 2005 as compared with April 2005?

V   W   X   Y   Z

Answer =

Q10. What was the percentage increase in the total sales of televisions in September 2005 as compared with April 2005?

42%   400%   500%   600%   5,000%

Answer =

The number of pupils who passed and failed GCE A level English examinations in five schools from 2001 to 2005:

School	Examination results	2001	2002	2003	2004	2005
1	Passed	25	19	21	16	28
	Failed	8	7	9	5	10
2	Passed	7	6	7	15	13
	Failed	4	4	5	9	7
3	Passed	4	4	4	6	3
	Failed	2	3	5	4	2
4	Passed	12	12	11	25	15
	Failed	6	5	6	11	8
5	Passed	8	9	13	17	16
	Failed	5	4	6	6	7

Q11. What was the total number of pupils who attempted the GCE A level English examination in 2001 and 2002?

197   154   200   128   225

Answer =

Q12. In which year did more pupils fail than pass the GCE A level English examination at School 3?

2001   2002   2003   2004   2005

Answer =

Q13. Which school had its least number of passes in GCE A level English in 2003 followed by its greatest number of passes in 2004?

1   2   3   4   5

Answer =

Q14. Of the total number of pupils who passed the GCE A level English examination in 2005, what percentage was from School 4?

7   10   15   17   20

Answer =

Q15. What was the ratio of the number of pupils who failed the GCE A level English examination in School 3 in 2002 to the number who passed it in School 2 in 2004?

1:6   1:5   1:4   4:15   1:3

Answer =

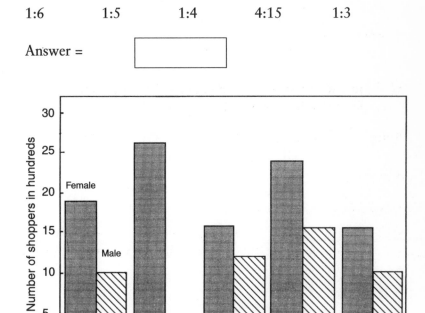

Figure 6.2   The number (in hundreds) of female and male shoppers on 1 June 2005 at five shops (V, W, X, Y and Z)

Q16. Which shop had the greatest number of shoppers on 1 June 2005?

V   W   X   Y   Z

Answer =

Q17. Which two of these five shops had the same number of male shoppers on 1 June 2005?

V   W   X   Y   Z

Answer =

Q18. What was the total number (in thousands) of female shoppers in these five shops on 1 June 2005?

10   15   50   100   10,000

Answer =

Q19. What proportion of the total number of male shoppers in these five shops on 1 June 2005 was at Shop Z?

$\frac{1}{20}$ $\frac{1}{15}$ $\frac{8}{75}$ $\frac{1}{5}$ $\frac{8}{25}$

Answer =

Q20. On 5 June 2005, the number of women and men shoppers in Shop Y increased by 25 per cent and 100 per cent respectively over the number of shoppers on 1 June 2005. What was the total number of shoppers (in hundreds) in Shop Y on 5 June 2005?

30   40   46   60   70

Answer =

Test 2

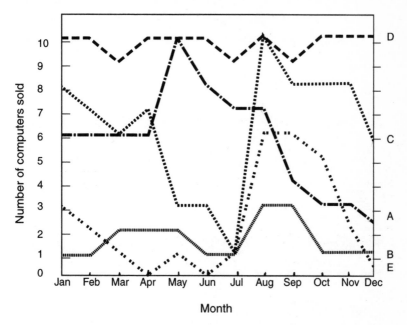

Figure 6.3   The number of computers sold by five salespeople (A, B, C, D and E) in each month of 2005

Q1.   Which person's computer sales were the most consistent throughout the year?

A   B   C   D   E

Answer =

Q2.   Which salesperson sold the same number of computers
      in each of four consecutive months?

A   B   C   D   E

Answer =   [   ]

Q3.   In which month did three of the salespeople sell the same
      number of computers?

March   April   May   July   August

Answer =   [   ]

Q4.   In which month did the computer sales of person C and
      person A differ most?

May   June   July   October   November

Answer =   [   ]

Q5.   Which month showed the largest increase in total
      computer sales over the total computer sales one month
      before?

April   May   July   August   November

Answer =   [   ]

Average length of the working week (in hours) for full-time employees in selected EU countries by employment sectors:

Country	Agriculture		Industry		Services	
	Men	Women	Men	Women	Men	Women
A	42.9	38.9	38.6	37.4	40.1	37.7
B	47.5	43.8	41.5	40.7	41.1	38.4
C	50.4	45.4	44.8	39.9	45.2	40.2
D	41.4	39.3	40.2	39.4	40.6	38.3
E	41.2	38.7	39.2	38.8	39.7	39.1
EU average	43.7	40.9	40.8	39.5	41.1	38.6

Q6. In which of the five countries do women work the longest hours when averaged across all three of the employment sectors (Agriculture, Industry and Services)?

A   B   C   D   E

Answer =

Q7. How much longer (in hours) is the average length of the working week for men compared with women across the five countries in the industrial sector?

0.80   1.25   1.62   1.75   1.84

Answer =

Q8. In which of the five countries does the average working
week of males in full-time employment in Agriculture
come closest to the EU average for females in that sector?

A   B   C   D   E

Answer =

Q9. What is the difference (in hours) between the average
length of the working week of men employed in
Agriculture across the five countries and the EU average
for men working in that sector?

0.70   0.84   0.98   1.24   1.37

Answer =

Q10. Which of the five countries comes closest to the EU
average for the duration of the working week in the
Service sector when the hours worked by both men and
women are taken into consideration?

A   B   C   D   E

Answer =

The number of residents at five hotels on 1 February and 1 July 2005:

1 February 2005

Hotel	Female adults	Male adults	Female children	Male children
V	32	64	8	11
W	11	28	3	2
X	47	84	14	7
Y	22	42	5	6
Z	63	104	18	23

1 July 2005

Hotel	Female adults	Male adults	Female children	Male children
V	41	73	16	14
W	18	37	7	6
X	47	92	12	17
Y	37	59	19	13
Z	81	112	26	20

Q11. Which of the five hotels had the same number of female adult residents on 1 February 2005 as it did on 1 July 2005?

V   W   X   Y   Z

Answer =

Q12. In which hotel was the total number of adult residents on
1 July 2005 three times greater than the total number of
children in residence?

V   W   X   Y   Z

Answer =

Q13. The number of male adult residents at one hotel on 1
February 2005 was 7 times its number of female children
residents on 1 July. Which hotel was it?

V   W   X   Y   Z

Answer =

Q14. Which hotel had the greatest increase in the total number
of adult residents on 1 July 2005 compared with 1
February of that year?

V   W   X   Y   Z

Answer =

Q15. What was the percentage increase in the total number of
female adult residents in all five hotels on 1 July 2005
compared with 1 February 2005?

28%   17%   49%   25%   31%

Answer =

Cinema admissions and takings in Great Britain 1969–79:

Number of admissions (millions)

1969	1970	1971	1972	1973	1974	1975	1976	1977	1978	1979
215	193	176	157	134	138	116	104	103	126	112

Average price of admission (pence)

1969	1970	1971	1972	1973	1974	1975	1976	1977	1978	1979
26.8	30.6	34.2	37.9	43.2	50.1	61.2	73.0	82.6	93.7	113.4

Regional analysis of admissions (for selected regions):

	Admissions (thousands)		Average price of admission (pence)	
	1978	1979	1978	1979
Great Britain	126,146	111,859	93.7	113.4
North Yorkshire	6,531	5,774	92.7	97.9
Yorkshire & Humberside	9,115	7,972	89.0	108.5
East Midlands	5,929	5,290	85.8	102.5
East Anglia	4,001	3,502	88.0	106.3
South-East:				
Greater London Council area	26,629	23,815	124.1	151.8
Outer Metropolitan area	13,200	11,763	85.3	103.7
West Midlands	8,083	7,765	83.8	100.9

Q16. In which year did the maximum increase in the average price of cinema admissions in Great Britain occur when compared with the previous year?

1973   1975   1977   1978   1979

Answer =

Q17. In 1970, the average price of cinema admissions in Great Britain was 30.6 pence. By which year had the average price increased by exactly 100 per cent?

1972   1973   1974   1975   1976

Answer =

Q18. What was the average annual decrease in cinema admissions (in millions) in Great Britain between 1969 and 1979?

9.36   103,000   1.03   10.30   103

Answer =

Q19. What percentage (approximately) of the total cinema admissions in Great Britain in 1978 was in the Greater London Council area of the South-East?

27%   12%   21%   25%   31%

Answer =

Q20. What would the average price in pence of cinema admissions in Great Britain in 1979 have been if the Greater London Council and the Outer Metropolitan areas of the South-East region had been excluded from the calculation?

115.2   103.2   105.2   106.3   104.5

Answer =

Test 3

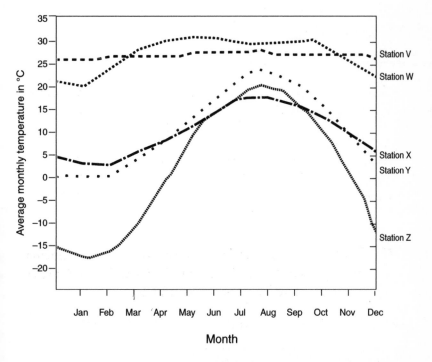

Figure 6.4 The average monthly temperatures (in degrees centigrade) for five weather stations in the northern hemisphere

Q1. Which of the five weather stations has the smallest annual range of temperature (ie the difference between the average temperature of its coldest month and its warmest month)?

V   W   X   Y   Z

Answer =

Q2. In which of the five weather stations is the average monthly temperature 1 degree centigrade higher in December than it is in January?

V   W   X   Y   Z

Answer =

Q3. Assume that plants begin to grow when the average monthly temperature rises above 6 degrees centigrade and ceases when the average monthly temperature falls below that figure. This period of plant growth is known as the 'growing season'. Which of the five stations has the shortest growing season?

V   W   X   Y   Z

Answer =

Q4. What is the ratio of months with average monthly
     temperatures of 5 degrees centigrade and below to those
     with average monthly temperatures above 5 degrees
     centigrade at Station Y?

1:4   3:12   1:2   5:7   3:9

Answer =

Q5. What is the average monthly temperature in degrees
     centigrade for January for all five weather stations
     combined?

13.6   7.4   4.8   −7.4   10.0

Answer =

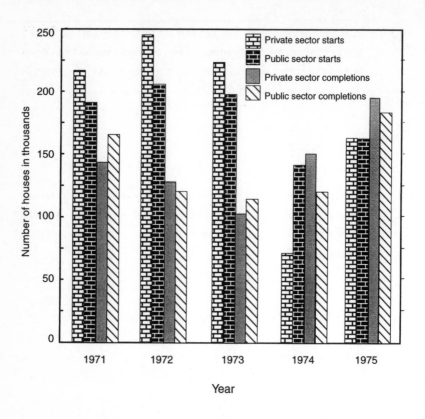

Figure 6.5   Number of houses built by different sectors in the United Kingdom, 1971–75

Q6.   In which of the five years in the period 1971–75 did the greatest number of private sector housing starts occur?

1971   1972   1973   1974   1975

Answer =

Q7. In which two of the five years during the period 1971–75 were the same number of public sector houses completed?

1971   1972   1973   1974   1975

Answer =

Q8. What was the total number (in thousands) of private sector housing completions in the five-year period 1971–75?

9,100   9,100,000   900   710   910

Answer =

Q9. What was the percentage (to the nearest per cent) increase in private sector housing starts from 1971 to 1972?

9%   14%   22%   19%   100%

Answer =

Q10. What proportion of the total number of housing starts in 1974 was in the public sector?

½   ⅓   ⅖   ⅗   ⅔

Answer =

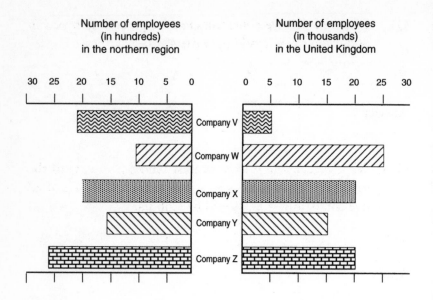

Figure 6.6   Number of employees in five companies in the United Kingdom (in thousands) and in the North (in hundreds)

Q11. What is the total number of employees (in thousands) in the United Kingdom of Company Z?

22.5   2,250   20,250   20   20,000

Answer =

Q12. How many (in thousands) of the United Kingdom employees of Company X work in regions outside the northern region?

1,800   20   18   18,000   2,000

Answer =

Q13. Which of the five companies has the greatest proportion of its employees working in the northern region?

V   W   X   Y   Z

Answer =

Q14. What percentage (to the nearest whole per cent) of the total number of employees in the United Kingdom of all five companies is employed by Company W?

58%   18%   23%   29%   34%

Answer =

Q15. If the total number of employees in the United Kingdom of Company X was to increase by 20 per cent and Company Y by 80 per cent, what would be the total combined workforce (in thousands) of the two companies?

46   51   54   59   62

Answer =

Number of new female and male employees engaged by five employers in 2001-05:

Employer	Gender of new employees	2001	2002	2003	2004	2005
V	Female	4	4	5	11	12
	Male	7	6	7	15	15
W	Female	10	11	9	17	15
	Male	12	12	11	25	14
X	Female	87	68	71	58	93
	Male	88	79	87	85	88
Y	Female	5	7	6	11	10
	Male	6	4	8	14	20
Z	Female	2	2	3	3	3
	Male	4	4	2	6	3

Q16. What was the total number of new employees (female and male) in all five companies in 2001 and 2002?

322   348   392   422   448

Answer =

Q17. Which of the five companies took on a bigger total of new employees in 2002 than in 2001?

V   W   X   Y   Z

Answer =

Q18. What was the average number of new female employees per company in 2004?

11   17   20   22   25

Answer =

Q19. Of the total number of new male employees in all five companies in 2005, what percentage was employed collectively by companies V, W and Y?

31%   35%   39%   41%   45%

Answer =

Q20. What was the ratio of new female employees in Company Y in 2001 to the number of new male employees in Company X in 2004?

1:15   3:29   1:17   6:85   1:19

Answer =

Test 4

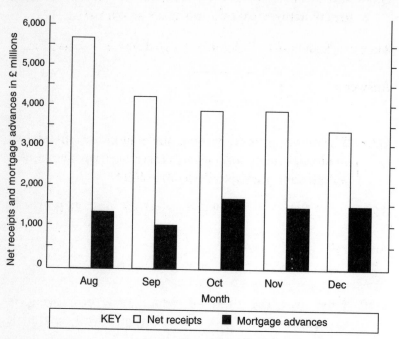

Figure 6.7 Building society net receipts and mortgage advances (in £ millions), August–December 2004

Q1. In which two of the five months were the same amount of building society mortgage advances made?

August   September   October   November   December

Answer =

Q2. In which month was there the greatest excess of building
society net receipts over mortgage advances?

August   September   October   November   December

Answer =

Q3. What was the total amount (in millions of pounds) of
building society mortgage advances over the five-month
period from August to December 2004?

6,200   7,000   70,000,000   7,800   78,000

Answer =

Q4. What was the ratio of building society mortgage
advances to net receipts in December 2004?

1:8   1:6   1:4   2:3   3:7

Answer =

Q5. Assume that, by the end of January 2005, the building
society net receipts and mortgage advances had fallen by
50 per cent and 25 per cent respectively compared with
the figures for December 2004. What would the building
society turnover (the figure obtained by adding net
receipts to mortgage advances) have been for January
2005 (in millions of pounds)?

1,800   2,875   24,000,000   2,400   24,000

Answer =

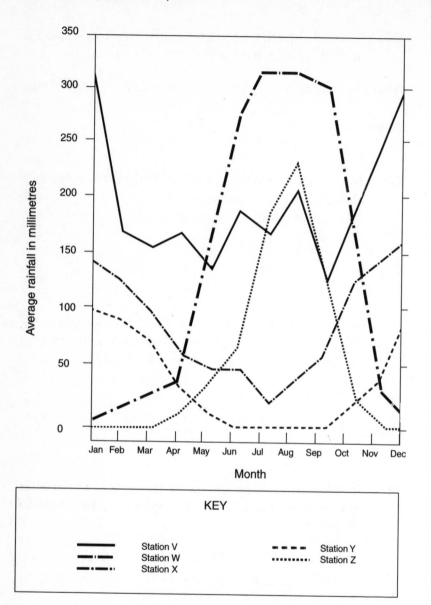

Figure 6.8 Average monthly rainfall in millimetres at five weather stations in the northern hemisphere

Q6.   In which month at Station V does the lowest average monthly rainfall total occur?

March   May   July   September   November

Answer =

Q7.   In how many months at Station Z is the average monthly rainfall total 0 millimetres?

3   4   5   6   7

Answer =

Q8.   In which of the five weather stations does the average monthly rainfall exceed 150 millimetres from May to October?

V   W   X   Y   Z

Answer =

Q9.   In which of the five weather stations does the average monthly rainfall fall below 50 millimetres for 8 months of the year?

V   W   X   Y   Z

Answer =

Q10. In which of the five weather stations is there the greatest difference between the month with the lowest average rainfall total and the month with the largest average rainfall total?

V   W   X   Y   Z

Answer =

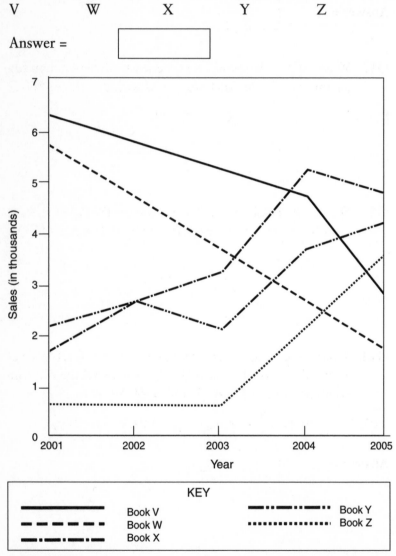

Figure 6.9 Sales (in thousands) of five books during the period 2001–05

Q11. Which of the five books had uniform sales for 3 years before increasing for the next 2 years at a constant rate?

V   W   X   Y   Z

Answer =

Q12. Which of the five books had the least difference between its annual sales in 2001 compared with its sales in 2005?

V   W   X   Y   Z

Answer =

Q13. What was the difference (in thousands) between the total sales for all five books in 2002 compared with 2004?

1.5   1,500   4   4.5   4,500

Answer =

Q14. What percentage (approximately) of the total annual sales for all five books in 2001 was contributed by the combined sales of Book V and Book Y?

33%   39%   45%   50%   55%

Answer =

Q15. What proportion (approximately) of the total annual
    sales for the period 2001-05 of Book W occurred in
    2003?

$\frac{1}{5}$ $\frac{2}{5}$ $\frac{1}{4}$ $\frac{2}{9}$ $\frac{1}{6}$

Answer =   [   ]

Service industry grants by regions in 1974 and 1977:

| Region | Year | Applications submitted | | Value (in | Number |
		Number submitted	Number offered	thousands of pounds)	of jobs created
V	1974	14	6	66	134
	1977	12	3	14	15
W	1974	19	5	155	211
	1977	25	8	56	43
X	1974	7	1	28	21
	1977	32	13	828	455
Y	1974	26	11	221	495
	1977	29	17	2,012	1,302
Z	1974	5	0	0	0
	1977	38	14	315	801

Q16. Which of the five regions had the greatest difference
    between the number of grant applications that it
    submitted in 1974 compared with 1977?

V   W   X   Y   Z

Answer =   [   ]

Q17. What was the difference between the total number of grant applications submitted by the five regions in 1974 compared with 1977?

58   65   69   76   80

Answer =

Q18. What was the average value (in thousands of pounds) per region of the service industry grants given to the five regions in 1977?

615   630   640,000   645   650

Answer =

Q19. Of the total number of jobs it was estimated that the service industry grants would create in the five regions in 1974, what proportion was it estimated would be in Region X?

$\frac{1}{34}$ $\frac{1}{40}$ $\frac{1}{41}$ $\frac{1}{43}$ $\frac{1}{47}$

Answer =

Q20. In which of the five regions in 1977 was the average cost per job created by means of service industry grants the highest?

V   W   X   Y   Z

Answer =

Number sequence tests

The number sequence tests provided here are similar to ones that are used in personnel selection in order to assess a candidate's understanding of the relationships between numbers, and how number systems work. The aim of this chapter, therefore, is to help you to develop your numerical reasoning, and to further your understanding of the principles on which number sequence items are based. In turn, this should help to improve your performance if and when you are required to take a test of this kind. However, before you tackle the practice tests you should take a look at the sample questions given below.

Sample questions

These tests differ from the previous test items in this book in that no words are used to tell you what you have to do – apart from the initial instructions. This is because number sequence problems are abstract – they are simply about numbers, the relationships between them and the different ways in which they can be manipulated. No attempt has been made to put the problems into real-world contexts, because the setters are not interested in testing your skills in the application of number in concrete situations. Hence you will find that what you are given to work with in each item has been pared down to the bare essentials, ie the information you need to be able to work out the answer – but no more. The questions, therefore, consist of a line of numbers with one number missing. You will find that this has been replaced with an 'xx', indicating that in all cases the answer is a double-digit number. Your task is to study the line of numbers in order to detect the pattern that lies hidden within the sequence – to 'crack the code'. Once you have done that, you should be able to calculate the missing number so as to arrive at the correct answer. With regard to the calculations, these will usually be additions, subtractions, multiplications and divisions – in some cases with two of them working in combination with each other. All of the numbers are whole numbers – so there are no fractions or decimals to worry about. Now take a look at the sample questions and try to work out the answers – it might be an idea to cover up the explanations given below whilst you do so!

Q1.   3   7   11   xx   19

Answer | xx = |

Q2.   1   2   4   8   xx

Answer | xx = |

Q3.   6   1   7   12   3   15   2   10   xx

Answer | xx = |

When you think that you know the answers, go back over the questions making a note of the 'rule' by which each item is constructed, ie the pattern hidden in the sequence of numbers. Then check out your answers and how you arrived at them with the ones given below:

In Q1, the numbers increase by +4:

$$3 (+ 4) = 7 (+ 4) = 11 (+ 4) = 15 (+ 4) = 19$$

The missing number (or xx), therefore, is 15.

In Q2, the numbers increase by a factor of 2, as follows:

$$1 (\times 2) = 2 (\times 2) = 4 (\times 2) = 8 (\times 2) = 16$$

The missing number (or xx), therefore, is 16.

In Q3, the numbers are in groups of three and, in each group of three, the second number added to the first equals the third. So:

$$6 + 1 = 7; 12 + 3 = 15; 2 + 10 = 12$$

The missing number (or xx), therefore, is 12.

Worked examples of common number sequence problems

Now that you have an idea as to what is involved in this type of numeracy test, it is time to take a close look at some worked examples of common types of number sequence problems. You should study them carefully because it will help you to recognize them when you see them again – and hence to know how to work them out correctly.

Example 1

3   10   xx   24   31

Answer | xx = 17 |

In this problem each number in the sequence is increased by a number that remains the same for each increase:

3 (+ 7) = 10 (+ 7) = **17** (+ 7) = 24 (+ 7) = 31

A variation will occur when each number in the sequence is decreased by a number that remains the same for each decrease – in this case by 4:

24   20   16   xx   8

Answer | xx = 12 |

24 (– 4) = 20 (– 4) = 16 (– 4) = **12** (– 4) = 8

Example 2

22   12   10   35   xx   16   34   23   11

Answer | xx = 19 |

The format of this problem is that the numbers are in groups of three, and the number on the right is taken away from the number on the left to give the number in the middle, ie:

22 – 10 = 12; 35 – 16 = **19**; 34 – 11 = 23

Variations on this basic formula occur when the position of the 'xx' is varied, thus altering the numerical calculation, eg:

xx   14   16   27   9   18   32   8   24

Answer $\boxed{\text{xx} = 30}$

30 (– 16) = 14; 27 (– 18) = 9; 32 (– 24) = 8

36   12   24   21   7   14   18   10   xx

Answer $\boxed{\text{xx} = 8}$

36 (– 24) = 12; 21 (– 14) = 7; 18 (– 8) = 10

Example 3

2   4   12   xx   240

Answer $\boxed{\text{xx} = 48}$

In this problem each number is increased by a constantly increasing multiple factor 2, 3, 4 and 5 as follows:

2 (× 2) = 4 (× 3) = 12 (× 4) = **48** (× 5) = 240

A variation in this type of problem occurs when each number is divided by a number that constantly decreases, eg:

480   96   xx   8   4

Answer $\boxed{\text{xx} = 24}$

480 (÷ 5) = 96 (÷ 4) = **24** (÷ 3) = 8 (÷ 2) = 4

Example 4

7   15   23   26   26   23   xx   7

Answer | xx = 15

In this problem the numbers are in a 'mirror pattern', ie the numbers to the left of the bar up to 26 are repeated on the right but in reverse order as follows:

7   15   23   26 | 26   23   15   7

Example 5

6230   83   1472   59   3152   xx   9061   97

Answer | xx = 47

In this problem there are two groups of numbers, one of four numbers (call them a, b, c and d) and the other of two numbers (e and f). The first two numbers (a + b) are added to find e, and the second two numbers (c + d) are added to find f, as follows:

$(6 + 2 = 8)(3 + 0 = 3) = 83; (1 + 4 = 5)(7 + 2 = 9) = 59; (3 + 1 = 4)(5 + 2 = 7) = 47$

Example 6

108   93   82   71   71   xx   93   108

Answer | xx = 82

This is another example of a 'mirror pattern' in the number sequence, ie the numbers to the left of the bar are repeated in reverse order on the right-hand side as follows:

108   93   82   71 | 71   **82**   93   108

Example 7

5   11   23   47   xx

Answer | xx = 95 |

In this problem the numbers are increased by a constant multiple factor plus 1 $(2n + 1)$ as follows:

$5 (\times 2 + 1) = 11 (\times 2 + 1) = 23 (\times 2 + 1) = 47 (\times 2 + 1) = \mathbf{95}$

Example 8

17   9   16   12   14   15   xx   18   7

Answer | xx = 11 |

This problem is an example of a 'hop a number' sequence. In fact, there are two sequences with alternate numbers following different rules as follows:

$17 (-1) = 16 (-2) = 14 (-3) = \mathbf{11} (-4) = 7$; and
$9 (+3) = 12 (+3) = 15 (+3) = 18$

Example 9

9   27   28   xx   85   255

Answer $\boxed{\text{xx} = 84}$

In this problem alternate numbers are increased in different ways. If you look closely at the sequence you will see that the first, third and fifth numbers are multiplied by a constant factor (in this case × 3) and that the second and fourth numbers are increased by the addition of a constant number (in this case + 1).

9 (× 3) = 27 (+ 1) = 28 (× 3) = 84 (+ 1) = 85 (× 3) = 255

Variations can occur when the alternate numbers in the sequence are multiplied and subtracted as follows:

9   27   26   78   xx   231

Answer $\boxed{\text{xx} = 77}$

9 (× 3 = 27 (– 1) = 26 (× 3) = 78 (– 1) = 77 (× 3) = 231

Similarly, alternate numbers can be changed by dividing and adding, eg:

64   32   36   18   22   xx

Answer $\boxed{\text{xx} = 11}$

64 (÷ 2) = 32 (+ 4) = 36 (÷ 2) = 18 (+ 4) = 22 (÷ 2) = 11

Alternate numbers can also be divided and subtracted, eg:

92   46   44   xx   20   10

Answer   xx = 22

$92 (\div 2) = 46 (-2) = 44 (\div 2) = 22 (-2) = 20 (\div 2) = 10$

Example 10

11   9   18   16   32   xx

Answer   xx = 30

This is a further variation of examples where alternate numbers in the sequence are treated differently. In this case the sequence is subtraction and then multiplication as follows:

$11 (-2 = 9 (\times 2) = 18 (-2) = 16 (\times 2) = 32 (-2) = 30$

Example 11

840   168   xx   14   7

Answer   xx = 42

In this case the numbers in the sequence are divided by a number that decreases by 1 as follows:

$840 (\div 5) = 168 (\div 4) = 42 (\div 3) = 14 (\div 2) = 7$

Example 12

124   16   592   61   xx3   20   416   47

Answer | xx = 17 |

The sequence in this problem consists of a group of three numbers followed by a pair of numbers – a pattern that is repeated. In the three-number groups, the first two numbers make up one double-digit number and the third is a single-digit number. When these two are added together they produce a two-digit number – the next pair in the sequence. This is how it works out with this example:

12 + 4 = 16; 59 + 2 = 61; **17** + 3 = 20; 41 + 6 = 47

Notice that, in order to calculate the missing number, 3 had to be subtracted from 20. A variation occurs when the 'xx' is placed in a different position in the sequence, as in the example given below. This has the effect of altering the type of numerical calculation that is required – in the case given below 6 being added to 24 to arrive at the missing number:

246   xx   328   40   227   29   514   55

Answer | xx = 30 |

24 + 6 = **30**; 32 + 8 = 40; 22 + 7 = 29; 51 + 4 = 55

Another variant to this type of problem occurs when subtractions are substituted for additions, as in the following example:

246   xx   328   24   227   15   514   47

Answer | xx = 18 |

24 – 6 = **18**; 32 – 8 = 24; 22 – 7 = 15; 51 – 4 = 47

Example 13

xx   27   26   42   14   28   54   11   43

Answer
$$\boxed{xx = 53}$$

In this type of problem the numbers are in groups of three. To calculate the answer the middle number has to be added to the third number in order to find the first number as follows:

$53 = 27 + 26;\ 42 = 14 + 28;\ 54 = 11 + 43$

Example 14

24   19   15   xx   10

Answer
$$\boxed{xx = 12}$$

In this type of problem the numbers are being changed in sequence by the deduction of a number that is reduced by 1 each time, as follows:

$24\ (-5) = 19\ (-4) = 15\ (-3) = \mathbf{12}\ (-2) = 10$

Example 15

216   54   xx   9

Answer
$$\boxed{xx = 18}$$

In this problem the numbers are divided by a number (starting with 4) that decreases by one for each successive calculation; the division of the first number (216) by 4 produces the second number (54), which when divided by 3 gives 18 – a number that, when divided by 2, produces the final number in the sequence (9):

$$216 (\div 4) = 54 (\div 3) = 18 (\div 2) = 9$$

Example 16

217   14   184   14   417   34   385   xx

Answer | xx = 33 |

This problem consists of groups of three numbers, with each group of three being followed by a pair of numbers. When the third number in a group of three is subtracted from the first two (treated as a two-digit number), it produces the number to the right as follows:

$$21 - 7 = 14; 18 - 4 = 14; 41 - 7 = 34; 38 - 5 = 33$$

A variant of this type of problem is given below. As you will see, in this case the groups of numbers are the same but the process is one of addition rather than subtraction.

648   72   374   41   622   xx   381   39

Answer | xx = 64 |

$$64 + 8 = 72; 37 + 4 = 41; 62 + 2 = 64; 38 + 1 = 39$$

Example 17

47　22　25　36　14　22　27　15　xx

Answer　　　　　| xx = 12 |

In this type of problem the numbers are in groups of three, and the middle number is subtracted from the first number (the one on the left) to find the third, as follows:

47 – 22 = 25; 36 – 14 = 22; 27 – 15 = **12**

Example 18

3　5　9　17　xx

Answer　　　　　| xx = 33 |

In problems of this kind, two processes are involved – the numbers are first multiplied by 2, and then 1 is subtracted from the resultant number to give the next number in the sequence, as follows:

3 (× 2) – 1 = 5 (× 2) – 1 = 9 (× 2) – 1 = 17 (× 2) – 1 = **33**

However, it should be noted that the same result can be obtained by using the following method:

3 + 2 = 5 + 4 = 9 + 8 = 17 + 16 = 33

Example 19

4216   67   2531   74   6151   76   6132   xx

Answer | xx = 75 |

In this problem the numbers are arranged in alternate groups of four and two – the latter deriving from the former as follows:

$(4 + 2)(1 + 6) = 67$; $(2 + 5)(3 + 1) = 74$; $(6 + 1)(5 + 1) = 76$; $(6 + 1)(3 + 2) = 75$

In other words, the first two numbers are added to give the tens and the second two to give the units of the two-digit numbers.

Example 20

6   6   8   12   12   24   20   xx   36

Answer | xx = 48 |

This is a problem in which alternate numbers in the sequence are increasing by a factor of 2 as follows:

$(6 \times 2) = 12$; $(12 \times 2) = 24$; $(24 \times 2) = 48$

Notice that in this example the other numbers in the sequence are also increasing but this time at a rate of twice the previous difference, as follows:

$6 (+ 2) = 8 (+ 4) = 12 (+ 8) = 20 (+ 16) = 36$

Number sequence practice tests

Each practice test consists of **30 questions** – you should aim to complete the final test in 12 minutes. Speed and accuracy are the key to success in this type of test – so in order to develop these skills we suggest that you allow yourself **15 minutes** for **Test 1**, **14 minutes** for **Test 2**, **13 minutes** for **Test 3** and **12 minutes** for **Test 4**. Before you begin, take a careful look at the following guidelines:

- Adhere strictly to the time limits suggested above.
- Mark your answers and give yourself a score out of 30 for each test – the answers are given on pages 193–203.
- After you have marked a test, go back over the items, jotting down how you arrived at your answers.
- Then compare your methods with the explanations given on pages 193–203, bearing in mind that there may be alternative ways of solving a problem.
- If at any stage you run into difficulties, go through the worked examples again to remind yourself of the principles on which items of this kind are constructed.

Test 1

Q1.   3   10   xx   24   31

Answer   xx =

Q2.   24   19   15   xx   10

Answer   xx =

Q3. 2   4   12   xx   240

Answer   xx = [   ]

Q4. 7   15   23   26   26   23   xx   7

Answer   xx = [   ]

Q5. 3   5   9   17   xx

Answer   xx = [   ]

Q6. 108   93   82   71   71   xx   93   108

Answer   xx = [   ]

Q7. 5   11   23   47   xx

Answer   xx = [   ]

Q8. 8   17   35   xx   143

Answer   xx = [   ]

Q9. 9   27   28   xx   85   255

Answer   xx = [   ]

Q10. 11   9   18   16   32   xx

Answer | xx = |

Q11. 217   14   184   14   417   34   385   xx

Answer | xx = |

Q12. 18   24   28   36   36   28   xx   18

Answer | xx = |

Q13. 124   16   592   61   xx   3   20   416   47

Answer | xx = |

Q14. 628   54   311   30   627   55   298   xx

Answer | xx = |

Q15. xx8   72   374   41   262   28   381   39

Answer | xx = |

Q16. 216   54   xx   9

Answer | xx = |

Q17. 840   168   xx   14

Answer | xx = |

Q18. 22   12   10   35   xx   16   34   23   11

Answer | xx = |

Q19. xx   27   26   42   14   28   54   11   43

Answer | xx = |

Q20. 47   22   25   36   14   22   27   15   xx

Answer | xx = |

Q21. 6230   83   1472   59   3152   xx   9061   97

Answer | xx = |

Q22. 4216   67   2531   74   6151   76   6132   xx

Answer | xx = |

Q23. 6   6   8   12   12   24   20   xx   36

Answer | xx = |

Q24. 17   9   16   12   14   15   xx   18   7

Answer   xx =

Q25. 38   26   28   56   56   28   xx   38

Answer   xx =

Q26. 432   108   xx   18

Answer   xx =

Q27. 206   14   195   14   429   33   366   xx

Answer   xx =

Q28. 547   61   274   31   722   xx   251   26

Answer   xx =

Q29. 7   9   13   21   xx

Answer   xx =

Q30. 8   17   35   xx   143

Answer   xx =

Test 2

Q1.   7   12   17   xx   27

Answer   xx =

Q2.   22   21   19   16   xx

Answer   xx =

Q3.   1   2   6   xx   120

Answer   xx =

Q4.   47   43   32   27   27   32   43   xx

Answer   xx =

Q5.   6   13   27   xx   111

Answer   xx =

Q6.   8   11   16   25   29   29   xx   16

Answer   xx =

Q7.   54   46   42   xx   39

Answer   xx =

Q8.   12   23   45   xx   177

Answer $\boxed{xx = \qquad}$

Q9.   4   8   9   18   19   xx

Answer $\boxed{xx = \qquad}$

Q10. 615   56   374   33   219   xx   417   34

Answer $\boxed{xx = \qquad}$

Q11. 12   9   27   24   72   xx

Answer $\boxed{xx = \qquad}$

Q12. 382   36   571   56   489   xx   593   56

Answer $\boxed{xx = \qquad}$

Q13. 127   19   594   63   xx8   25   406   46

Q14. xx7   53   301   29   727   65   290   29

Answer $\boxed{xx = \qquad}$

Q15. 1320   264   66   xx

Answer   xx =

Q16. 23   11   12   35   xx   16   34   13   21

Answer   xx =

Q17. xx   27   16   52   24   28   34   11   23

Answer   xx =

Q18. 46   22   68   39   10   49   27   15   xx

Answer   xx =

Q19. 6234   87   1872   99   2122   xx   8061   87

Answer   xx =

Q20. 2216   47   2634   87   7172   89   6232   xx

Answer   xx =

Q21. 6   7   14   15   30   xx

Answer   xx =

Q22. 8   24   23   xx   68   204

Answer   xx =

Q23. 16   8   14   16   10   xx   2   192

Answer   xx =

Q24. 26   84   29   72   35   60   47   xx

Answer   xx =

Q25. 628   54   311   30   627   55   298   xx

Answer   xx =

Q26. 4   10   16   xx   28

Answer   xx =

Q27. 48   12   36   55   xx   26   36   13   23

Answer   xx =

Q28. 3   6   xx   72   360

Answer   xx =

Q29. 9   xx   28   36   36   28   17   9

Answer | xx = |

Q30. 240   xx   12   4   2

Answer | xx = |

Test 3

Q1.   4   7   10   xx   16

Answer | xx = |

Q2.   16   24   xx   40   48

Answer | xx = |

Q3.   38   36   32   xx   8

Answer | xx = |

Q4.   60   44   36   32   xx

Answer | xx = |

Q5.   80   60   42   xx   12

Answer | xx = |

Q6.   16   20   28   44   xx

Answer   xx =

Q7.   7   9   13   16   17   17   16   xx

Answer   xx =

Q8.   8   17   35   xx   143

Answer   xx =

Q9.   4   9   19   39   xx

Answer   xx =

Q10. 4   6   12   14   15   15   xx   12

Answer   xx =

Q11. 8   15   29   xx   113

Answer   xx =

Q12. 10   19   37   xx   145

Answer   xx =

Q13. 24   29   36   41   41   36   xx   24

Answer   xx =

Q14. 197   12   865   81   263   xx   412   39

Answer   xx =

Q15. 583   55   627   55   196   13   xx4   34

Answer   xx =

Q16. 193   22   318   39   327   xx   506   56

Answer   xx =

Q17. 199   28   156   21   xx5   48   462   48

Answer   xx =

Q18. 62   27   35   48   17   31   39   12   xx

Answer   xx =

Q19. 83   14   69   37   xx   15   56   19   37

Answer   xx =

Q20. 27   16   11   xx   11   18   49   21   28

Answer | xx = |

Q21. 26   13   39   34   xx   57   19   17   36

Answer | xx = |

Q22. 2563   79   8123   95   2624   xx   7025   77

Answer | xx = |

Q23. 3   5   20   22   88   xx   360

Answer | xx = |

Q24. 1851   96   1652   77   3152   xx   8140   94

Answer | xx = |

Q25. 4252   67   4362   xx   5322   84   6145   79

Answer | xx = |

Q26. 6   xx   27   55   111

Answer | xx = |

Q27. 17   8   16   12   15   xx   14   20

Answer   xx =

Q28. 8   24   25   xx   76   228   229

Answer   xx =

Q29. 98   xx   48   46   23

Answer   xx =

Q30. xx   34   27   43   14   29   68   43   25

Answer   xx =

Test 4

Q1.   17   24   xx   38   45

Answer   xx =

Q2.   21   30   39   xx   57

Answer   xx =

Q3.   10   16   xx   28   34

Answer   xx =

Q4. 74 71 65 53 xx

Answer   xx =

Q5. 80 70 61 53 xx

Answer   xx =

Q6. 57 49 42 xx 31

Answer   xx =

Q7. 9 19 39 xx 159

Answer   xx =

Q8. 7 15 31 xx 127

Answer   xx =

Q9. 11 23 47 xx 191

Answer   xx =

Q10. 9 17 33 xx 129

Answer   xx =

Q11. 7   13   25   49   xx

Answer   xx =

Q12. 12   23   45   xx   177

Answer   xx =

Q13. 191   18   468   38   514   47   301   xx

Answer   xx =

Q14. 624   58   326   26   152   13   377   xx

Answer   xx =

Q15. 265   21   486   42   625   xx   427   35

Answer   xx =

Q16. 478   55   182   20   264   xx   305   35

Answer   xx =

Q17. 625   67   324   36   471   xx   247   31

Answer   xx =

Q18. 376   43   295   34   587   xx   365   41

Answer   xx =

Q19. 45   17   28   49   xx   20   28   11   17

Answer   xx =

Q20. 58   11   47   38   xx   23   82   43   39

Answer   xx =

Q21. 35   24   11   46   xx   22   66   27   39

Answer   xx =

Q22. 24   16   40   46   27   73   61   29   xx

Answer   xx =

Q23. 64   18   82   16   xx   35   37   49   86

Answer   xx =

Q24. 77   14   91   41   18   59   18   xx   37

Answer   xx =

Q25. 8036   89   3372   69   5231   xx   1132   25

Answer   xx =

Q26. 3471   78   4213   64   4126   58   2417   xx

Answer   xx =

Q27. 8132   95   2433   66   2216   xx   1426   58

Answer   xx =

Q28. 3478   4589   23xx   1256

Answer   xx =

Q29. 3467   1245   45xx   2356

Answer   xx =

Q30. 1618   1921   2224   25xx

Answer   xx =

Answers and explanations

Chapter 4: Number problem tests

Test 1

Q1. *Answer:* A
Explanation: 408 ÷ 8 = 51 × 2 = 102

Q2. *Answer:* C
Explanation: £4.40 + £2.75 = £7.15

Q3. *Answer:* C
Explanation: 05.30 + 9.0 = 14.30

Q4. *Answer:* E
Explanation: £3.50 × 3 = £10.50

Q5. *Answer:* E
Explanation: 23p + £2.35 + £10.40 = £12.98

Q6. *Answer:* A
Explanation: 35 + 55 min = 90 min = 1½ hours

Q7. *Answer:* C
Explanation: 14.15 – 06.00 = 8 hours 15 min or 8¼ hours

Q8. *Answer:* B
Explanation: $5 \times 120 = 600$

Q9. *Answer:* D
Explanation: $550 \div 2 = 275$

Q10. *Answer:* D
Explanation: $660 \div 10 = 10\% = 66 \times 2 = 20\% = 132$

Q11. *Answer:* C
Explanation: £110 × 12 = £1,320

Q12. *Answer:* B
Explanation: $72.5 - 50 = 22.5$ mph

Q13. *Answer:* D
Explanation: $3 \times 7 = 21$

Q14. *Answer:* D
Explanation: $13,750 \div 10 = 10\% = 1,375 \times 9 = 90\% = 12,375$

Q15. *Answer:* D
Explanation: $18 \div 3 = 6$ mph

Q16. *Answer:* E
Explanation: $13.30 + 9 = 22.30$

Q17. *Answer:* B
Explanation: 12,500 cm $\div 100 = 125 \div 1 = 125$

Q18. *Answer:* B
Explanation: $2 \times 2 = 4$ sq m; $40 \times 40 = 1,600$ sq m $\div 4 = 400$

Q19. *Answer:* C
Explanation: 23p × 7 = £1.61

Q20. *Answer:* D
Explanation: £4 ÷ 8 = 50p × 3 = £1.50

Q21. *Answer:* D
Explanation: $100 \div 8 = 12.5\%$

Q22. *Answer:* C
Explanation: 125 × 12 = 1,500

Q23. *Answer:* B
Explanation: 40 ÷ 4.5 = 8.88

Q24. *Answer:* D
Explanation: 300 ÷ 30 = 10 ounces; 105 × 10 = 1,050

Q25. *Answer:* A
Explanation: 97 × 1.6 = 155.2 = 155 km

Test 2

Q1. *Answer:* C
Explanation: £10 – £2.73 = £7.27

Q2. *Answer:* A
Explanation: 14.30 – 06.30 = 8 × 7 = 56

Q3. *Answer:* B
Explanation: £110 ÷ 100 = £1.1 × 5 = 5% = £5.50 + £110 = £115.50

Q4. *Answer:* D
Explanation: £8 = ¼ of £32; ¼ of 100% = 25%

Q5. *Answer:* D
Explanation: £46.00 ÷ 2 = £23.00

Q6. *Answer:* C
Explanation: 1,180 ÷ 2 = 590

Q7. *Answer:* B
Explanation: 90 ÷ 30 = 3

Q8. *Answer:* D
Explanation: 7 × 3 = 21; 4.5 × 2.5 = 11.25; 21 + 11.25 = 32.25

Q9. *Answer:* A
Explanation: 100 ÷ 40 = 2½ hours; 100 ÷ 80 = 1¼ hours; 2½ + 1¼ = 3¾

Q10. *Answer:* D
Explanation: 10 – 9 = 1; 10 = 100%; therefore 1 = 10%

Q11. *Answer:* C
Explanation: ½ m = 50 cm ÷ 2 cm = 25

Q12. *Answer:* D
Explanation: £3,500 + £6,700 + £7,800 = £18,000 ÷ 3 = £6,000

Q13. *Answer:* C
Explanation: 1% of £2.00 = 2p; 40p ÷ 2p = 20p = 20%

Q14. *Answer:* C
Explanation: 29 + 27 + 33 = 89

Q15. *Answer:* B
Explanation: 120 m + 189 m = 309 m

Q16. *Answer:* D
Explanation: 8 min × 26 = 208 min

Q17. *Answer:* B
Explanation: 2,420 ÷ 220 = 11

Q18. *Answer:* D
Explanation: 1% of £8 = 8p; 20 ÷ 8 = 2.5

Q19. *Answer:* B
Explanation: 75 ÷ 3 = 25; 75 – 25 = 50

Q20. *Answer:* C
Explanation: 24 ÷ 3 × 2 = 16 × 5 = 80

Q21. *Answer:* E
Explanation: 7.6 × 20 = 152

Q22. *Answer:* B
Explanation: 26.5 × 9 = 238.5 ÷ 5 = 47.7 + 32 = 79.7

Q23. *Answer:* D
Explanation: Cost/sq m = £110 ÷ 5 = £22; area = 3 × 2.5 = 7.5;
cost = £22 × 7.5 + £35 = £200

Q24. *Answer:* C
Explanation: Taxi = £8 + drinks = £9.60 + food = £24.40 = £42
÷ 4 = £10.50

Q25. *Answer:* D
Explanation: 7.5 × 2 × 2 = 30.00 ÷ 5 = 6

Test 3

Q1. *Answer:* D
Explanation: 60 × 10 = 600; 30 × 5 = 150; 600 ÷ 150 = 4;
1 litre ÷ 4 = 0.25

Q2. *Answer:* D
Explanation: £3.43 + £1.52 = £4.95; £7.37 – £4.95 = £2.42

Q3. *Answer:* C
Explanation: 92 m ÷ 4.7 = 19.57 = 19

Q4. *Answer:* D
Explanation: 1% of £140 = £1.40 × 2.5 = £3.50

Q5. *Answer:* B
Explanation: 50 × 2.5 = 125 ÷ 25 = 5 × 20 = 100

Q6. *Answer:* B
Explanation: 24 × 4 = 96; 8 + 10½ + 6 + 11 = 35½; 96 – 35½
= 60½

Q7. *Answer:* A
Explanation: 2.01 + 1.92 + 1.57 + 1.88 + 2.05 = 9.43 ÷ 5 =
1.886 m = 188.6 cm

Q8. *Answer:* A
Explanation: 1% of £160 = £1.60 × 8 = 8% = £12.80 + £160 =
£172.80

Q9. *Answer:* B
Explanation: 84 × 84 = 7,056; 7 × 7 = 49; 7,056 ÷ 49 = 144

Q10. *Answer:* D
Explanation: 67.5 mph – 40 mph = 27.5 mph

Q11. *Answer:* B
Explanation: £12 × 5 = £60

Q12. *Answer:* A
Explanation: 57 × 7 = 399

Q13. *Answer:* B
Explanation: £352.00 × 4 = £1,408.00

Q14. *Answer:* C
Explanation: 420 miles ÷ 7 hours = 60 mph

Q15. *Answer:* E
Explanation: £37.00 – £21.32 = £15.68

Q16. *Answer:* D
Explanation: 117 ÷ 9 = 13

Q17. *Answer:* A
Explanation: £213 ÷ 3 = £71

Q18. *Answer:* C
Explanation: 1% of 500 = 5 × 6 = 6% = 30 + 500 = 530

Q19. *Answer:* E
Explanation: 18 ÷ 24 = ¾ = 75%

Q20. *Answer:* E
Explanation: 10% of £230 = £23 × 4 = 40% = £92 × 2 = £184

Q21. *Answer:* B
Explanation: 2,498 – 1,004 = 1,494 = male members; ratio = 1,494:1,004 = 1,500:1,000 (approx); divide both by 500 = 3 to 2

Q22. *Answer:* D
Explanation: 100% ÷ 8 × 5 = 62.5%

Q23. *Answer:* C
Explanation: 92 + 30 = 122; 1% of workforce = 6; 122 ÷ 6 = 20% approx

Q24. *Answer:* B
Explanation: 7 m × 5 m = 35 sq m; 2 m × 2 m = 4 sq m; 35 sq m − 4 sq m = 31 sq m

Q25. *Answer:* C
Explanation: 783 × 8.4p ÷ 100 = £65.77 + £15.75 = £81.52

Test 4

Q1. *Answer:* C
Explanation: Perimeter of park = 500 m × 4 = 2,000 m ÷ 100 m = 20

Q2. *Answer:* C
Explanation: 13 m × 13 m = 169 sq m ÷ 2 = 84.5 sq m

Q3. *Answer:* A
Explanation: 18 + 23 + 41 + 37 = 119 ÷ 4 = 29.75

Q4. *Answer:* B
Explanation: 4 out of 8 (= ½) over 40; 100% ÷ 2 = 50%

Q5. *Answer:* D
Explanation: £12.43 − £7.67 = £4.76

Q6. *Answer:* B
Explanation: 50 mph + 23 mph = 73 mph

Q7. *Answer:* E
Explanation: £14.46 + 6 × 50p = £17.46 ÷ 6 = £2.91

Q8. *Answer:* B
Explanation: 450 − 90 = 360 ÷ 15 = 24

Q9. *Answer:* C
Explanation: 5 × 24 = 120

Q10. *Answer:* A
Explanation: 13.15 – 04.30 = 8¾ × 5 = 43¾ hours

Q11. *Answer:* B
Explanation: 60 + 75 + 25 + 40 + 50 = 250 ÷ 5 = 50 mph

Q12. *Answer:* E
Explanation: 1% of 1,244 = 12.44 × 25 = 311

Q13. *Answer:* D
Explanation: 67.5 ÷ 9 = 7½ hours

Q14. *Answer:* D
Explanation: £29.99 + £23.50 + £18.00 = £71.49; £120 – £71.49 = £48.51

Q15. *Answer:* B
Explanation: 1% of £160 = £1.60 × 12.5 = £20; £160 – £20 = £140

Q16. *Answer:* C
Explanation: £45 + £105 = £150; 1% of £150 = £1.50 × 17.5 = £26.25 + £150 = £176.25

Q17. *Answer:* B
Explanation: 24 + 24 + 9 + 9 = 66 m ÷ 3 m = 22

Q18. *Answer:* E
Explanation: £2.50 × 5 = £12.50; £140 – £12.50 = £127.50

Q19. *Answer:* D
Explanation: 35 × £6 = £210; 6 × £12 = £72 + £210 = £282

Q20. *Answer:* D
Explanation: 35 × 6½ = 227.5 miles

Q21. *Answer:* B
Explanation: £35 + £45 + £55 + £250 = £385; 1% of £385 = £3.85 × 15 = £57.75; £385 – £57.75 = £327.25

Q22. *Answer:* C
Explanation: 150 out of 500 = 30%; 225 out of 500 = 45%;
45 − 30 = 15%

Q23. *Answer:* D
Explanation: Total of journey times 25 + 25 + 30 etc = 260 min
÷ 10 = 26 min

Q24. *Answer:* E
Explanation: 80 cm × 20 cm × 2.5 cm = 4,000 cubic centimetres

Q25. *Answer:* B
Explanation: £25 ÷ £5 = 5; £200 ÷ £20 = 10; £200 ÷ £10 = 20;
5 + 10 + 20 = 35

Chapter 5: Data interpretation tests (1)

Test 1

Q1. *Answer:* 290
Explanation: June: 10 + 23 + 46 + 22 + 16 + 18 = 135
July: 12 + 20 + 58 + 24 + 15 + 26 = 155
June + July = 155 + 135 = 290

Q2. *Answer:* B
Explanation: Sub-station B attended 42 emergencies in August compared to 20 in July = an increase of 22 = the largest increase

Q3. *Answer:* B
Explanation: Total emergencies for each station over the five-month period:
A = 86; B = 135; C = 125; D = 120; E = 78; F = 134

Q4. *Answer:* 26%
Explanation: 43 emergencies attended by C in September out of a total of 165 attended by all six sub-stations: 43 divided by 165 and multiplied by 100 gives a figure of 26.06%, rounded to 26%

Q5. *Answer:* April
Explanation: In April, the difference of 10% in the amount of support between B and E was the largest difference between parties over the six-month period

Q6. *Answer:* A and C
Explanation: The totals of the percentage support for A and C over the six-month period were both 124

Q7. *Answer:* B and E
Explanation: The percentage of the vote given to A becomes 12 (24 ÷ 2); B remains 25; C becomes 21 (18 + 3); D becomes 20 (17 + 3); E becomes 22 (16 + 6)

Q8. *Answer:* 850
Explanation: To calculate 17% of 5,000: 5,000 ÷ 100 = 50 (or 1%); 50 × 17 = 850

Q9. *Answer:* A and D
Explanation: The total number of sales for shops A and D = 169

Q10. *Answer:* 7
Explanation: Total sales in shop C = 180 items. We know that one assistant sold 36 items, so 180 − 36 = 144. The other shop assistants sold 24 items each, so dividing 144 by 24 = 6, which is the number of other shop assistants. 6 + 1 = 7

Q11. *Answer:* B
Explanation: The total sales for each shop become: A = 149 (169 − 20); B = 158; C = 90 (180 ÷ 2); D = 141 (169 − 28); E = 126

Q12. *Answer:* £1,265
Explanation: 22 trainers sold at an average sales price of £57.50: 22 × £57.50 = £1,265

Q13. *Answer:* C and E
Explanation: The proportion of income received from public funds and research contracts by C was 74% (54 + 20), the same as E (58 + 16)

Q14. *Answer:* D
Explanation: The proportion of total income received by D from research contracts (19%), investments (19%) and vacation lettings (7%) was 45%, ie above any of the other universities

Q15. *Answer:* C
Explanation: The proportion of total income received by C from investments (12%) and donations (2%) was 14%, ie below any of the other universities

Q16. *Answer:* £2,009,000
Explanation: To calculate 7% of £28.7 million: 1% = £28,700,000 ÷ 100 = £287,000 × 7 = 7% = £2,009,000

Q17. *Answer:* A and F
Explanation: In 2004, the unemployment rate in A (5.5%) had increased by 1.3% compared with 2000 (4.2%); the unemployment rate in F had also increased by 1.3% in 2004 (8.1%) compared with 2000 (6.8%)

Q18. *Answer:* 0.1
Explanation: The total of the unemployment rates in 2004 was: 5.5 + 4.6 + 5.0 + 9.0 + 6.8 + 8.1 = 39

The total of the unemployment rates in 2003 was: 5.3 + 4.3 + 5.6 + 9.4 + 6.3 + 7.5 = 38.4

39 – 38.4 = 0.6 ÷ 6 (countries) = 0.1

Q19. *Answer:* 3
Explanation: The average unemployment rate in the two countries was:

D – 8.7 + 9.0 + 9.2 + 9.4 + 9.0 = 45.3

E – 5.4 + 5.9 + 5.9 + 6.3 + 6.8 = 30.3

45.3 – 30.3 = 15 ÷ 5 (number of years) = 3

Q20. *Answer:* 195,000
Explanation: There was an increase of 0.3% in the number of unemployed in country D in 2004 compared with 2000 (9.00 – 8.7 = 0.3). To calculate 0.3% of 65 million: 65,000,000 ÷ 100 × 0.3 = 195,000

Test 2

Q1. *Answer:* B
Explanation: B = 100 – 41 = 59% of households not owning microwaves (A = 52%; C = 51%; D = 54%; E = 57%)

Q2. *Answer:* 12
Explanation: (11 + 4) + (7 + 4) + (11 + 5) + 10 + 8 = 60 ÷ 5 = 12

Q3. *Answer:* 16.6
Explanation: (100 – 82) + (100– 85) + (100 – 87) + (100 – 83) + (100 – 80) = 83 ÷ 5 = 16.6

Q4. *Answer:* D and E
Explanation: Total crime figure for D is 319 – 160 (fraud) = 159; total crime figure for E is 274 – 115 (fraud) = 159

Q5. *Answer:* 721
Explanation: Total crime figure for B in first quarter is 350; increased by 6% to 371 in second quarter; 350 + 371 = 721

Q6. *Answer:* 306
Explanation: Total of robberies is 333; 92% of 333 = 306.4 or 306 (rounded)

Q7. *Answer:* A and C
Explanation: Totals of both Class A and Class C are £162

Q8. *Answer:* 17
Explanation: 162 – 18 (Tracey) = 144 ÷ 9 (amount raised by others) = 16 + Tracey = 17

Q9. *Answer:* Jumble sale
Explanation: The total for the jumble sale becomes £124. This is above the income from other events

Q10. *Answer:* 26%
Explanation: The total amount raised by Class E is £122. £32 was raised through the jumble sale. 32 ÷ 122 × 100 = 26 (rounded)

Q11. *Answer:* –6
Explanation: 4 commodities (beverages, cereals, fats and oils, and minerals) changed in value by a total of –58 points; the other 2 (timber and metal) changed in value by +22 points; difference between –58 and +22 = –36; average = –36 ÷ 6 = –6

Q12. *Answer:* Beverages
Explanation: The drop in the value of beverages from 95 to 76 was greater than any other change

Q13. *Answer:* Minerals
Explanation: The change in the value of minerals of –6 points was the smallest change from 2000 to 2004

Q14. *Answer:* £6,120
Explanation: £180 × 12 (months) × 20 (years) = £43,200 – £37,080 (£206 × 12 × 15) = £6,120

Q15. *Answer:* £37,950
Explanation: 126.50 × 12 × 25 = £37,950

Q16. *Answer:* £2,400
Explanation: £135 × 12 × 20 = £32,400 – £30,000 (£125 × 12 × 20) = £2,400

Q17. *Answer:* £51.12
Explanation: 8.8% of £340 = £29.92 + £21.20 (10.6% of £200) = £51.12

Q18. *Answer:* 2003/2004
Explanation: The sum of the percentage increases of the six items in 2003 compared to 2002 is 10.4% = the same as the sum of the percentage increases in 2004 compared to 2003

Q19. *Answer:* £217.64
Explanation: The price of a television set in 2004 is £265 + 9.5% = £290.18; 25% off £290.18 = £72.54; £290.18 – £72.54 = £217.64

Q20. *Answer:* £3.63
Explanation: Vacuum cleaner price in 2001 is £131 (£125 + 4.8%). Price in 2003 is £134.63 (£125 + 7.7%). £134.63 – £131 = £3.63

Test 3

Q1. *Answer:* 22.7
Explanation: The percentage total in chemistry is 77.3%. 100 – 77.3 = 22.7

Q2. *Answer:* English
Explanation: When percentage passing at each grade (A–E) is added together for each subject, English has the highest total (85.2%) compared with the next highest (Geography = 78.6%)

Q3. *Answer:* 1,100
Explanation: 11.9% of 46,540 = 5,538 – 4,456 (10.5% of 42,440) = 1,082

Q4. *Answer:* 6,926
Explanation: 24% (failed to obtain grades) of 28,860 (28,860 ÷ 100 × 24) = 6,926

Q5. *Answer:* 2 and 3
Explanation: The total for both years (2 and 3) is 525

Q6. *Answer:* Wheat and maize
Explanation: Both commodities (wheat and maize) dropped by $38

Q7. *Answer:* +5
Explanation: 165 – 12% = 145 + 528 (503 + 5%) = 673 – 668
= +5

Q8. *Answer:* £50
Explanation: 7th to 17th = 11 days; £12.50 × 4 = £50

Q9. *Answer:* £135
Explanation: 7th to 14th = 8 days at £15 × 3 adults = £45 × 3
(winter sports) = £135

Q10. *Answer:* £279.30
Explanation: 14-day holiday at the Worldwide rate: 3 at
£24.50 (2 adults and one child aged 15) = £73.50 × 3 (winter
sports) = £220.50 + £58.8 (20% discount for child under 14) =
£279.30

Q11. *Answer:* £101.20
Explanation: Premium of £22.00 increased by 15% = £25.30 ×
4 = £101.20

Q12. *Answer:* £57.80
Explanation: £50 + 15.6% (£7.80) = £57.80

Q13. *Answer:* +£0.80
Explanation: The Green family spends 15% more on clothing:
15% of £22 = £3.30; it spends 5% less on food: 5% of £50 =
£2.50; £3.30 – £2.50 = £0.80. Since spending on all other items
is the same, the difference = +£0.80

Q14. *Answer:* £187
Explanation: £214 + 25% = £267.50 – £59.11 (£46 + 28.5%)
– £21.76 (£18 + 20.9%) = £186.63 = £187 (rounded)

Q15. *Answer:* Housing
Explanation: Housing increase of 20.1% (28.5 – 8.4)

Q16. *Answer:* Red and Green
Explanation: Both Red and Green troops raised £111

Q17. *Answer:* 7
Explanation: Total raised by Green Troop is £111 – £27 (Leroy) = £84 ÷ 14 = 6 + 1 = 7

Q18. *Answer:* Raffle
Explanation: Red Troop raffle income becomes £7.50 and the raffle total income £84.50, ie the highest

Q19. *Answer:* £147
Explanation: Total amount raised is £533 – £386 (wheelchair) = £147

Q20. *Answer:* £109.20
Explanation: Total amount raised by Brown Troop is £91; 20% of £91 = £18.20; £91 + £18.20 = £109.20

Test 4

Q1. *Answer:* £1,950
Explanation: 36 repayments at £331.94 = £11,949.84 – £10,000 = £1,949.84 = £1,950 (rounded)

Q2. *Answer:* £1,630
Explanation: There are 12 months' repayments outstanding at £135.80 = £1,629.60 = £1,630 (rounded)

Q3. *Answer:* £1,300
Explanation: (£220.83 × 60) – (£331.94 × 36) = £1,299.96 = £1,300 (rounded)

Q4. *Answer:* £6,500
Explanation: (£441.67 × 60) – £20,000 = £6,500 (rounded)

Q5. *Answer:* £938
Explanation: (£291 × 2) + (£178 × 2) = £938

Q6. *Answer:* £580
Explanation: (£320 × 4) − (£175 × 4) = £580

Q7. *Answer:* £249
Explanation: 3(£222 + 12%) − 2(£222 + 12%) = £249 (rounded)

Q8. *Answer:* £700
Explanation: 2(£156 + 8%) + 2(£162 + 12%) = £700 (rounded)

Q9. *Answer:* C
Explanation: £22.12 (C) = lowest total

Q10. *Answer:* Beef
Explanation: Lowest price £7.80 to highest price £8.90

Q11. *Answer:* £1.13
Explanation: In A, beef increases by 5%; 5% of £8.90 = £0.445; new price = £8.90 + £0.445 = £9.345; 2 kilos = £9.345 × 2 = £18.69. In A, butter decreases by 10%; 10% of £4.60 = £0.46; new price = £4.60 − £0.46 = £4.14; 2 kilos = £4.14 × 2 = £8.28. Cost in A = £18.69 + £8.28 = £26.97. Cost in C = £8.10 (price of beef per kilo) × 2 = £16.20 + £4.82 (price of butter) × 2 = £9.64. Cost in C = £16.20 + £9.64 = £25.84. Difference = £26.97 − £25.84 = £1.13

Q12. *Answer:* £20.56
Explanation: Total of cheapest items (eg beef at supermarket B = £7.80 and cheese at supermarket C = £4.95, etc) = £20.56

Q13. *Answer:* 1,711
Explanation: Dealer A sold 846 new cars in 2000 and 912 (846 + 66) in 2005; Dealer D sold 760 new cars in 2000 and 799 (760 + 39) in 2005; total of A and D in 2005 = 912 and 799 = 1,711

Q14. *Answer:* 800
Explanation: The sum of cars sold in 2000 + the sum of cars sold in 2003 ÷ 6 = 800

Q15. *Answer:* 450
Explanation: (8% of 866 = 69) + (10% of 3,808 = 381) = 449 = 450 (rounded)

Q16. *Answer:* F
Explanation: 57 ÷ 584 × 100 = 9.7% increase in sales

Q17. *Answer:* 12%
Explanation: 22 more emergencies attended in September; 22 ÷ 180 × 100 = 12.2% = 12% (rounded)

Q18. *Answer:* 11
Explanation: 249 (August total) − 185 (July total) ÷ 6 = 10.66 = 11

Q19. *Answer:* +12
Explanation: (36 + 25%) + (36 + 25%) + (38 − 16%) = 122 − 110 = +12

Q20. *Answer:* C and F
Explanation: Both stations (C and F) attended 191 emergencies

Chapter 6: Data interpretation tests (2)

Test 1

Q1. *Answer:* W
Explanation: Graph shows school W had most pupils (500) in 2001

Q2. *Answer:* 19
Explanation: Read off totals (in hundreds) for all five schools from the graph and then total them (= 19)

Q3. *Answer:* W
Explanation: Line for school W is the only one to decrease in a straight line

Q4. *Answer:* Z
Explanation: Line for school Z stays at the same level 2003–2005

Q5. *Answer:* Y
Explanation: Line for school Y rises each year from 2002 onwards

Q6. *Answer:* Z
Explanation: Shop Z sold 92 TVs and 92 radios

Q7. *Answer:* X
Explanation: Shop X sold 12 TVs and 14 DVDs – a difference of 2

Q8. *Answer:* V
Explanation: Shop V sold 120 DVDs in September and 20 TVs in April (6 × 20 = 120)

Q9. *Answer:* Z
Explanation: Shop Z sold 24 DVDs in April and 160 in September – a difference of 136 (more than any of the other shops)

Q10. *Answer:* 400%
Explanation: Total TV sales in the five shops in April = 84; total TV sales in the five shops in September = 420; 420 – 84 = increase of 336 ÷ 84 = 4 × 100% = 400%

Q11. *Answer:* 154
Explanation: Add number of students who passed and failed for all five schools for 2001; repeat process for 2002; add two totals together = 154

Q12. *Answer:* 2003
Explanation: 4 passed and 5 failed in School 3 in 2003

Q13. *Answer:* 4
Explanation: School 4 had its least number of passes in 2003 (11) and most in 2004 (25)

Q14. *Answer:* 20
Explanation: Total number of passes = 75 ÷ 15 (passes in School 4) = 5; 100% ÷ 5 = 20%

Q15. *Answer:* 1:5
Explanation: Number who failed in School 3 in 2002 = 3; number who passed in School 2 in 2004 = 15; 3:15 = 1:5

Q16. *Answer:* Y
Explanation: The column on the graph for women shoppers is second highest for Shop Y (2,400) and the highest for men (1,500), giving an overall total of 3,900, which is greater than that for any of the other shops

Q17. *Answer:* V and Z
Explanation: The two columns (V and Z) are at the same height on the graph, indicating that they had the same number of shoppers

Q18. *Answer:* 10
Explanation: The number of female shoppers for each shop can be extracted from the graph and the numbers can then be added up to give a total of 10,000. Question asks for the number in thousands, and hence the answer = 10

Q19. *Answer:* ⅕
Explanation: Number of male shoppers for each shop can be extracted from the graph and the numbers then added together (= 5,000). Number in Shop Z = 1,000. Ratio therefore = 1:5

Q20. *Answer:* 60
Explanation: Graph shows that the number of female shoppers = 24 and the number of male shoppers = 15 (both in hundreds); 25% of 24 = 24 ÷ 4 = 6; 24 + 6 = 30; increase of 15 by 100% = 15 × 2 = 30; 30 + 30 = 60

Test 2

Q1. *Answer:* D
Explanation: Graph shows that the line for D varies least from month to month

Q2. Answer: A
Explanation: Graph shows that A sold the same number of computers in the first four months (Jan–Apr)

Q3. *Answer:* July
Explanation: Graph shows that B, C and E sold the same number in July

Q4. *Answer:* May
Explanation: Graph shows greatest difference (gap) between sales figures for C and A was in May

Q5. *Answer:* August
Explanation: Graph shows that sales rose steeply for B, C, D and E from July to August

Q6. *Answer:* C
Explanation: Inspection of the data shows that there are two possibilities, B and C. Figures are as follows: B = 122.9 ÷ 3 = 40.96; C = 125.5 ÷ 3 = 41.83; therefore answer = C

Q7. *Answer:* 1.62
Explanation: Add hours worked by men in the five countries (= 204.3) and for women (= 196.2); divide both by 5 to get the average (= 40.86 and 39.24); difference = 1.62

Q8. *Answer:* E
Explanation: EU average for women employees in Agriculture = 40.9 hours. Country E, in which men in that sector work 41.2 hours, is closest, ie 0.3 hours more

Q9. *Answer:* 0.98
Explanation: Add figures for men in the five countries employed in Agriculture (42.9 + 47.5 + 50.4 + 41.4 + 41.2) = 223.4 ÷ 5 = 44.68 = average for five countries − 43.7 (EU average) = 0.98

Q10. *Answer:* B
Explanation: Men working in Services in B work 41.1 hours on average − the same as the EU average. Women work 38.4 hours compared with the EU average of 38.6

Q11. *Answer:* X
Explanation: X had 47 adult female residents on each of the two dates

Q12. *Answer:* Y
Explanation: Y had 96 adult residents (37 + 59) and 32 child residents (19 + 13); 96 ÷ 32 = 3

Q13. *Answer:* X
Explanation: X had 84 adult male residents on 1 February and 12 child female residents on 1 July; 84 ÷ 12 = 7

Q14. *Answer:* Y
Explanation: Y showed an increase from 64 adult residents on 1 February to 96 on 1 July − a number greater than any of the others

Q15. *Answer:* 28%
Explanation: Total number of female residents on 1 February = 175, on 1 July = 224; 175 ÷ 100 = 1.75 = 1%; 224 ÷ 1.75 = 128 = increase of 28%

Q16. *Answer:* 1979
Explanation: Greatest increase in average price of admissions occurred in 1979 from 1978, ie 93.7p to 113.4p

Q17. *Answer:* 1975
Explanation: 30.6p × 100% = 61.2p = the average price of admissions in 1975

Q18. *Answer:* 10.30
Explanation: Decrease in admissions (in millions) = 215 − 112
= 103; average annual decrease 1969–1979 = 103 ÷ 10 = 10.30
(million)

Q19. *Answer:* 21%
Explanation: Admissions in 1978: Great Britain = 126,146;
Greater London Council area = 26,629; 26,629 ÷ 126,146 ×
100 ÷ 1 = 21.1% or 21% (rounded)

Q20. *Answer:* 103.2
Explanation: Average price of admissions (in pence) in the five
regions added together = 516.1; therefore average price = 516.1
÷ 5 = 103.2

Test 3

Q1. *Answer:* V
Explanation: Graph shows temperature for Station V stays
close to 25°C throughout the year

Q2. *Answer:* X
Explanation: Graph shows Station X has a temperature of 5°C
in January and 6°C in December

Q3. *Answer:* Z
Explanation: A line across the graph at 6°C would show that
Station Z has fewer months above that temperature than any of
the others, ie the shortest growing season

Q4. *Answer:* 1:2
Explanation: A line across the graph at 5°C would show that
Station Y has 4 months below that temperature and 8 above it,
and hence a ratio of 4:8 or 1:2

Q5. *Answer:* 7.4
Explanation: Read off January temperatures in °C for all five
stations = Z −15, Y 0, X 5, W 10 and V 26; add temperatures
together and divide by 5 = 7.4

Q6. *Answer:* 1972
Explanation: Column for private sector starts was highest in 1972

Q7. *Answer:* 1972 and 1974
Explanation: Columns for public sector completions are at the same height in 1972 and 1974

Q8. *Answer:* 710
Explanation: Read off number of private sector completions (in thousands) for all five years and add them up; total = 710

Q9. *Answer:* 14%
Explanation: Rise = 30,000 (215,000 in 1971 to 245,000 in 1972); 215,000 ÷ 100 = 1% = 2,150; 30,000 ÷ 2,150 = 13.95 = 14% (to nearest whole percentage)

Q10. *Answer:* ⅔
Explanation: Graph shows that in 1974 housing starts in thousands were: public sector 140; private sector 70. Total (in thousands) = 140 + 70 = 210. Proportion of public sector starts to total starts = 140:210 = ⅔

Q11. *Answer:* 20
Explanation: Bar for Company Z shows that the number of employees (in thousands) in the UK is 20

Q12. *Answer:* 18
Explanation: Graph shows that Company X has 20 × 100 = 2,000 employees in the northern region out of 20,000 in the UK; employees in other regions therefore = 20,000 − 2,000 = 18,000. Answer in thousands = 18

Q13. *Answer:* V
Explanation: Company V has 2,100 employees in the northern region out of a total of 5,000 in the UK

Q14. *Answer:* 29%
Explanation: From the graph, total (in thousands) of employees in UK of all five companies = 85, of which Company W employs 25; 85 ÷ 100 = 0.85 = 1%; 25 ÷ 0.85 = 29.4 = 29% (to nearest whole percentage)

Q15. *Answer:* 51
Explanation: In thousands, Company X employs 20 and Company Y 15. For Company X, 20% of 20 = 20 ÷ 5 = 4 (= increase); new total = 20 + 4 = 24. For Company Y, 80% of 15 = 15 ÷ 5 × 4 = 12 (= increase); new total = 15 + 12 = 27. Total combined workforce (in thousands) = 24 + 27 = 51

Q16. *Answer:* 422
Explanation: Add up the numbers in the two columns headed 2001 and 2002 = 422

Q17. *Answer:* W
Explanation: Company W took on 22 (10 female and 12 male) new workers in 2001 and 23 (11 female and 12 male) in 2002 – other companies took on fewer or the same number

Q18. *Answer:* 20
Explanation: Add up number of new female employees in 2004 in all five companies = 100 ÷ 5 to get the average per company = 20

Q19. *Answer:* 35%
Explanation: Total number of new male employees in all five companies in 2005 = 140. Total number of new employees in companies V, W and Y = 49; 49 ÷ 140 × 100 ÷ 1 = 35%

Q20. *Answer:* 1:17
Explanation: Number of new female employees in Company Y in 2001 = 5; number of new male employees in Company X in 2004 = 85; ratio = 5:85 = 1:17

Test 4

Q1. *Answer:* November and December
Explanation: The columns for mortgage advances are the same height for November and December

Q2. *Answer:* August
Explanation: The difference in height between the receipts and the advances columns is greatest for the month of August

Q3. *Answer:* 7,000
Explanation: The monthly advances (in millions) are August £1,400, September £1,000, October £1,600, November £1,500 and December £1,500; therefore total = £1,400 + £1,000 + £1,600 + £1,500 + £1,500 = £7,000

Q4. *Answer:* 3:7
Explanation: Advances in December = £1,500 and net receipts = £3,500; ratio = 1,500:3,500 = 3:7

Q5. *Answer:* 2,875
Explanation: Receipts in December = 3,500 (in millions of pounds) and advances = 1,500; 50% of 3,500 = 1,750 and 75% of 1,500 = 1,125. Turnover for January 2005 = 1,750 + 1,125 = 2,875

Q6. *Answer:* September
Explanation: Line for Station V on graph falls to its lowest point in September

Q7. *Answer:* 4
Explanation: Line for Station Z is at 0 mm for December, January, February and March = 4

Q8. *Answer:* W
Explanation: The line for Station W rises above the 150 mm level in May and stays above it until October

Q9. *Answer:* Y
Explanation: The line for Station Y dips below the 50 mm level for 8 months

Q10. *Answer:* W
Explanation: The line for Station W rises from nearly 0 mm in January to 325 mm in July

Q11. *Answer:* Z
Explanation: The line on the graph for Book Z shows that its sales were constant in 2001, 2002 and 2003. It then rose in a straight line (indicating a constant rate of increase) in 2004 and 2005

Q12. *Answer:* Y
Explanation: Graph shows that sales for Book Y were 2,200 in 2001 and 4,300 in 2005 – a gap that is smaller than that of any of the other books

Q13. *Answer:* 1.5
Explanation: Read off the sales figures for each of the five books for the two years (2002 and 2004), add them up and then compare the two totals – the difference = 1.5 (in thousands)

Q14. *Answer:* 50%
Explanation: Graph shows that the sales (in thousands) of the five books in 2001 were as follows: V = 6.4, W = 5.8, X = 1.8, Y = 2.1 and Z = 0.7; total = 16.8; combined sales of V and Y = 8.5 = just over half of total for all five books; therefore answer = 50% (approx)

Q15. *Answer:* ⅕
Explanation: Graph shows the sales (in thousands) of Book W to have been as follows: 2001 = 5.8; 2002 = 4.8; 2003 = 3.8; 2004 = 2.6; 2005 = 1.8; total = 18.8; total for 2003 = 3.8; proportion = 3.8 to 18.8 = ⅕

Q16. *Answer:* Z
Explanation: Table shows that Region Z submitted 5 applications in 1974 and 38 in 1977 – a difference of 33 – a figure greater than that of any of the other regions

Q17. *Answer:* 65
Explanation: Total up allocations for 1974 (= 71) and 1977 (= 136); difference = 136 – 71 = 65

Q18. *Answer:* 645
Explanation: Total for five regions (in thousands of pounds) for 1977 = 3,225; to calculate average per region, divide by 5: 3,225 ÷ 5 = 645

Q19. *Answer:* $\frac{1}{41}$
Explanation: Total jobs created in all five regions in 1974 = 861; of those, 21 were created in Region X; 861/21 = 41; proportion = $\frac{1}{41}$

Q20. *Answer:* X
Explanation: In 1977, 455 jobs were created in Region X at a cost of 828 (in thousands of pounds). The cost per job = 828 ÷ 455 = 1.8 (thousand pounds) – a figure that is higher than for any of the other regions

Chapter 7: Number sequence tests

Test 1

Q1. *Answer:* 17
Explanation: 3 + 7 = 10 + 7 = **17** + 7 = 24 + 7 = 31

Q2. *Answer:* 12
Explanation: 24 – 5 = 19 – 4 = 15 – 3 = **12** – 2 = 10

Q3. *Answer:* 48
Explanation: 2 × 2 = 4 × 3 = 12 × 4 = **48** × 5 = 240

Q4. *Answer:* 15
Explanation: 7   15   23   26 | 26   23   **15**   7

Q5. *Answer:* 33
Explanation: $3 + 2 = 5 + 4 = 9 + 8 = 17 + 16 = 33$

Q6. *Answer:* 82
Explanation: 108   93   82   71 | 71   82   93   108

Q7. *Answer:* 95
Explanation: $5 \times 2 + 1 = 11 \times 2 + 1 = 23 \times 2 + 1 = 47 \times 2 + 1 = 95$

Q8. *Answer:* 71
Explanation: $8 \times 2 + 1 = 17 \times 2 + 1 = 35 \times 2 + 1 = 71 \times 2 + 1 = 143$

Q9. *Answer:* 84
Explanation: $9 \times 3 = 27 + 1 = 28 \times 3 = 84 + 1 = 85 \times 3 = 255$

Q10. *Answer:* 30
Explanation: $11 - 2 = 9 \times 2 = 18 - 2 = 16 \times 2 = 32 - 2 = 30$

Q11. *Answer:* 33
Explanation: $21 - 7 = 14; 18 - 4 = 14; 41 - 7 = 34; 38 - 5 = 33$

Q12. *Answer:* 24
Explanation: 18   24   28   36 | 36   28   24   18

Q13. *Answer:* 17
Explanation: $12 + 4 = 16; 59 + 2 = 61; 17 + 3 = 20; 41 + 6 = 47$

Q14. *Answer:* 21
Explanation: $62 - 8 = 54; 31 - 1 = 30; 62 - 7 = 55; 29 - 8 = 21$

Q15. *Answer:* 64
Explanation: $64 + 8 = 72; 37 + 4 = 41; 26 + 2 = 28; 38 + 1 = 39$

Q16. *Answer:* 18
Explanation: $216 \div 4 = 54 \div 3 = 18 \div 2 = 9$

Q17. *Answer:* 42
Explanation: $840 \div 5 = 168 \div 4 = \mathbf{42} \div 3 = 14$

Q18. *Answer:* 19
Explanation: $22 = 12 + 10$; $35 = \mathbf{19} + 16$; $34 = 23 + 11$

Q19. *Answer:* 53
Explanation: $\mathbf{53} = 27 + 26$; $42 = 14 + 28$; $54 = 11 + 43$

Q20. *Answer:* 12
Explanation: $47 - 22 = 25$; $36 - 14 = 22$; $27 - 15 = \mathbf{12}$

Q21. *Answer:* 47
Explanation: $(6 + 2 = 8$ and $3 + 0 = 3) = 83$; $(1 + 4 = 5$ and $7 + 2 = 9) = 59$; $(3 + 1 = 4$ and $5 + 2 = 7) = \mathbf{47}$; $(9 + 0 = 9$ and $6 + 1 = 7) = 97$

Q22. *Answer:* 75
Explanation: $(4 + 2 = 6$ and $1 + 6 = 7) = 67$; $(2 + 5 = 7$ and $3 + 1 = 4) = 74$; $(6 + 1 = 7$ and $5 + 1 = 6) = 76$; $(6 + 1 = 7$ and $3 + 2 = 5) = \mathbf{75}$

Q23. *Answer:* 48
Explanation: Alternate numbers: $6 \times 2 = 12 \times 2 = 24 \times 2 = \mathbf{48}$

Q24. *Answer:* 11
Explanation: Alternate numbers: $17 - 1 = 16 - 2 = 14 - 3 = \mathbf{11} - 4 = 7$

Q25. *Answer:* 26
Explanation: 38   26   28   56 | 56   28   **26**   38

Q26. *Answer:* 36
Explanation: $432 \div 4 = 108 \div 3 = \mathbf{36} \div 2 = 18$

Q27. *Answer:* 30
Explanation: $20 - 6 = 14$; $19 - 5 = 14$; $42 - 9 = 33$; $36 - 6 = \mathbf{30}$

Q28. *Answer:* 74
Explanation: $54 + 7 = 61$; $27 + 4 = 31$; $72 + 2 = 74$; $25 + 1 = 26$

Q29. *Answer:* 37
Explanation: 7 + 2 = 9 + 4 = 13 + 8 = 21 + 16 = **37**

Q30. *Answer:* 71
Explanation: 8 × 2 + 1 = 17 × 2 + 1 = 35 × 2+ 1 = **71** × 2 + 1 = 143

Test 2

Q1. *Answer:* 22
Explanation: 7 + 5 = 12 + 5 = 17 + 5 = **22** + 5 = 27

Q2. *Answer:* 12
Explanation: 22 − 1 = 21 − 2 = 19 − 3 = 16 − 4 = **12**

Q3. *Answer:* 24
Explanation: 1 × 2 = 2 × 3 = 6 × 4 = **24** × 5 = 120

Q4. *Answer:* 47
Explanation: 47   43   32   27 | 27   32   43   **47**

Q5. *Answer:* 55
Explanation: 6 × 2 + 1 = 13 × 2 + 1 = 27 × 2 + 1 = **55** × 2 + 1 = 111

Q6. *Answer:* 25
Explanation: 8   11   16   25   29 | 29   **25**   16

Q7. *Answer:* 40
Explanation: 54 − 8 = 46 − 4 = 42 − 2 = **40** − 1 = 39

Q8. *Answer:* 89
Explanation: 12 × 2 − 1 = 23 × 2 − 1 = 45 × 2 − 1 = **89** × 2 − 1 = 177

Q9. *Answer:* 38
Explanation: 4 × 2 = 8 + 1 = 9 × 2 = 18 + 1 = 19 × 2 = **38**

Q10. *Answer:* 12
Explanation: 61 − 5 = 56; 37 − 4 = 33; 21 − 9 = **12**; 41 − 7 = 34

Q11. *Answer:* 69
Explanation: $12 - 3 = 9$; $\times 3 = 27 - 3 = 24$; $\times 3 = 72 - 3 = \mathbf{69}$

Q12. *Answer:* 39
Explanation: $38 - 2 = 36$; $57 - 1 = 56$; $48 - 9 = \mathbf{39}$; $59 - 3 = 56$

Q13. *Answer:* 17
Explanation: $12 + 7 = 19$; $59 + 4 = 63$; $\mathbf{17} + 8 = 25$; $40 + 6 = 46$

Q14. *Answer:* 60
Explanation: $\mathbf{60} - 7 = 53$; $30 - 1 = 29$; $72 - 7 = 65$; $29 - 0 = 29$

Q15. *Answer:* 22
Explanation: $1{,}320 \div 5 = 264 \div 4 = 66 \div 3 = \mathbf{22}$

Q16. *Answer:* 19
Explanation: $23 - 12 = 11$; $35 - 16 = \mathbf{19}$; $34 - 21 = 13$

Q17. *Answer:* 43
Explanation: $\mathbf{43} = 27 + 16$; $52 = 24 + 28$; $34 = 11 + 23$

Q18. Answer: 42
Explanation: $46 + 22 = 68$; $39 + 10 = 49$; $27 + 15 = \mathbf{42}$

Q19. *Answer:* 34
Explanation: $(6 + 2 = 8$ and $3 + 4 = 7) = 87$; $(1 + 8 = 9$ and $7 + 2 = 9) = 99$; $(2 + 1 = 3$ and $2 + 2 = 4) = \mathbf{34}$; $(8 + 0 = 8$ and $6 + 1 = 7) = 87$

Q20. *Answer:* 85
Explanation: Sequence as in Q19; therefore $(6 + 2 = 8$ and $3 + 2 = 5) = \mathbf{85}$

Q21. *Answer:* 31
Explanation: $6 + 1 = 7 \times 2 = 14 + 1 = 15 \times 2 = 30 + 1 = \mathbf{31}$

Q22. *Answer:* 69
Explanation: $8 \times 3 = 24 - 1 = 23 \times 3 = \mathbf{69} - 1 = 68 \times 3 = 204$

Q23. *Answer:* 48
Explanation: Alternate numbers $8 \times 2 = 16 \times 3 = \mathbf{48} \times 4 = 192$

Q24. *Answer*: 48
Explanation: Alternate numbers $84 - 12 = 72 - 12 = 60 - 12 = 48$

Q25. *Answer*: 21
Explanation: $62 - 8 = 54; 31 - 1 = 30; 62 - 7 = 55; 29 - 8 = 21$

Q26. *Answer*: 22
Explanation: $4 + 6 = 10 + 6 = 16 + 6 = 22 + 6 = 28$

Q27. *Answer*: 29
Explanation: $48 - 12 = 36; 55 - 29 = 26; 36 - 13 = 23$

Q28. *Answer*: 18
Explanation: $3 \times 2 = 6 \times 3 = 18 \times 4 = 72 \times 5 = 360$

Q29. *Answer*: 17
Explanation: 9   **17**   28   36 | 36   28   17   9

Q30. *Answer*: 48
Explanation: $240 \div 5 = 48 \div 4 = 12 \div 3 = 4 \div 2 = 2$

Test 3

Q1. *Answer*: 13
Explanation: $4 + 3 = 7 + 3 = 10 + 3 = 13 + 3 = 16$

Q2. *Answer*: 32
Explanation: $16 + 8 = 24 + 8 = 32 + 8 = 40 + 8 = 48$

Q3. *Answer*: 24
Explanation: $38 - 2 = 36 - 4 = 32 - 8 = 24 - 16 = 8$

Q4. *Answer*: 30
Explanation: $60 - 16 = 44 - 8 = 36 - 4 = 32 - 2 = 30$

Q5. *Answer*: 26
Explanation: $80 - 20 = 60 - 18 = 42 - 16 = 26 - 14 = 12$

Q6. *Answer*: 76
Explanation: $16 + 4 = 20 + 8 = 28 + 16 = 44 + 32 = 76$

Q7. *Answer:* 13
Explanation: 7   9   13   16   17 | 17   16   **13**

Q8. *Answer:* 71
Explanation: $8 \times 2 + 1 = 17 \times 2 + 1 = 35 \times 2 + 1 = 71 \times 2 + 1$
$= 143$

Q9. *Answer:* 79
Explanation: $4 + 5 = 9 + 10 = 19 + 20 = 39 + 40 = $ **79**

Q10. *Answer:* 14
Explanation: 4   6   12   14   15 | 15   **14**   12

Q11. *Answer:* 57
Explanation: $8 \times 2 - 1 = 15 \times 2 - 1 = 29 \times 2 - 1 = 57 \times 2 - 1$
$= 113$

Q12. *Answer:* 73
Explanation: $10 \times 2 - 1 = 19 \times 2 - 1 = 37 \times 2 - 1 = 73 \times 2 - 1$
$= 145$

Q13. *Answer:* 29
Explanation: 24   29   36   41 | 41   36   **29**   24

Q14. *Answer:* 23
Explanation: $19 - 7 = 12; 86 - 5 = 81; 26 - 3 = \mathbf{23}; 41 - 2 = 39$

Q15. *Answer:* 38
Explanation: $58 - 3 = 55; 62 - 7 = 55; 19 - 6 = 13; \mathbf{38} - 4 = 34$

Q16. *Answer:* 39
Explanation: $19 + 3 = 22; 31 + 8 = 39; 32 + 7 = \mathbf{39}; 50 + 6 = 56$

Q17. *Answer:* 43
Explanation: $19 + 9 = 28; 15 + 6 = 21; \mathbf{43} + 5 = 48; 46 + 2 = 48$

Q18. *Answer:* 27
Explanation: $62 - 35 = 27; 48 - 31 = 17; 39 - \mathbf{27} = 12$

Q19. *Answer:* 22
Explanation: $83 - 69 = 14; 37 - 15 = \mathbf{22}; 56 - 37 = 19$

Q20. *Answer:* 29
Explanation: 27 – 16 = 11; **29** – 11 = 18; 49 – 21 = 28

Q21. *Answer:* 23
Explanation: 39 – 26 = 13; 57 – 34 = **23**; 36 – 19 = 17

Q22. *Answer:* 86
Explanation: (2 + 5 = 7 and 6 + 3 = 9) = 79; (8 + 1 = 9 and 2 + 3 = 5) = 95; (2 + 6 = 8 and 2 + 4 = 6) = **86**; (7 + 0 = 7 and 2 + 5 = 7) = 77

Q23. *Answer:* 90
Explanation: Alternate sequence 3 + 2 = 5 × 4 = 20 + 2 = 22 × 4 = 88 + 2 = **90** × 4 = 360

Q24. *Answer:* 47
Explanation: As Q22: (3 + 1 = 4 and 5 + 2 = 7) = **47**

Q25. *Answer:* 78
Explanation: As Q24: (4 + 3 = 7 and 6 + 2 = 8) = **78**

Q26. *Answer:* 13
Explanation: 6 × 2 + 1 = **13** × 2 + 1 = 27, repeated throughout the sequence; alternatively 6 + 7 = **13** + 14 = 27 + 28 = 55 + 56 = 111

Q27. *Answer:* 16
Explanation: Alternate numbers 17 – 1 = 16 – 1 = 15 and 8 + 4 = 12 + 4 = **16**, repeated throughout the sequence

Q28. *Answer:* 75
Explanation: 8 × 3 = 24 + 1 = 25 × 3 = **75** + 1 = 76 etc

Q29. *Answer:* 96
Explanation: Alternate numbers 98 – 2 = **96** ÷ 2 = 48 – 2 = 46 ÷ 2 = 23

Q30. *Answer:* 61
Explanation: **61** = 34 + 27; 43 = 14 + 29; 68 = 43 + 25

Test 4

Q1. *Answer:* 31
Explanation: $17 + 7 = 24 + 7 = \textbf{31} + 7 = 38 + 7 = 45$

Q2. *Answer:* 48
Explanation: $21 + 9 = 30 + 9 = 39 + 9 = \textbf{48} + 9 = 57$

Q3. *Answer:* 22
Explanation: $10 + 6 = 16 + 6 = \textbf{22} + 6 = 28 + 6 = 34$

Q4. *Answer:* 29
Explanation: $74 - 3 = 71 - 6 = 65 - 12 = 53 - 24 = \textbf{29}$

Q5. *Answer:* 46
Explanation: $80 - 10 = 70 - 9 = 61 - 8 = 53 - 7 = \textbf{46}$

Q6. *Answer:* 36
Explanation: $57 - 8 = 49 - 7 = 42 - 6 = \textbf{36} - 5 = 31$

Q7. *Answer:* 79
Explanation: $9 + 10 = 19 + 20 = 39 + 40 = \textbf{79} + 80 = 159$

Q8. *Answer:* 63
Explanation: $7 + 8 = 15 + 16 = 31 + 32 = \textbf{63} + 64 = 127$

Q9. *Answer:* 95
Explanation: $11 + 12 = 23 + 24 = 47 + 48 = \textbf{95} + 96 = 191$

Q10. *Answer:* 65
Explanation: $9 \times 2 - 1 = 17 \times 2 - 1 = 33 \times 2 - 1 = \textbf{65} \times 2 - 1 = 129$

Q11. *Answer:* 97
Explanation: $7 \times 2 - 1 = 13 \times 2 - 1 = 25 \times 2 - 1 = 49 \times 2 - 1 = \textbf{97}$

Q12. *Answer:* 89
Explanation: $12 \times 2 - 1 = 23 \times 2 - 1 = 45 \times 2 - 1 = \textbf{89} \times 2 - 1 = 177$

Q13. *Answer:* 29
Explanation: $19 - 1 = 18$; $46 - 8 = 38$, repeated through to $30 - 1 = 29$

Q14. *Answer:* 30
Explanation: $62 - 4 = 58$, repeated through to $37 - 7 = 30$

Q15. *Answer:* 57
Explanation: $26 - 5 = 21$, repeated through to $62 - 5 = 57$

Q16. *Answer:* 30
Explanation: $47 + 8 = 55$; $18 + 2 = 20$; $26 + 4 = 30$; etc

Q17. *Answer:* 48
Explanation: $62 + 5 = 67$, repeated through to $47 + 1 = 48$

Q18. *Answer:* 65
Explanation: $37 + 6 = 43$, repeated through to $58 + 7 = 65$

Q19. *Answer:* 29
Explanation: $45 - 28 = 17$; $49 - 20 = 29$; etc

Q20. *Answer:* 15
Explanation: $58 - 47 = 11$; $38 - 23 = 15$; etc

Q21. *Answer:* 24
Explanation: $35 - 24 = 11$; $46 - 24 = 22$; etc

Q22. *Answer:* 90
Explanation: $24 + 16 = 40$, repeated through to $61 + 29 = 90$

Q23. *Answer:* 19
Explanation: $64 + 18 = 82$; $16 + 19 = 35$; etc

Q24. *Answer:* 19
Explanation: $77 + 14 = 91$; $41 + 18 = 59$; $18 + 19 = 37$

Q25. *Answer:* 74
Explanation: $(8 + 0 = 8$ and $3 + 6 = 9) = 89$, repeated through to $(5 + 2 = 7$ and $3 + 1 = 4) = 74$

Q26. *Answer:* 68
Explanation: (3 + 4 = 7 and 7 + 1 = 8) = 78, repeated through to (2 + 4 = 6 and 1 + 7 = 8) = **68**

Q27. *Answer:* 47
Explanation: (8 + 1 = 9 and 3 + 2 = 5) = 95, repeated through to (2 + 2 = 4 and 1 + 6 = 7) = **47**

Q28. *Answer:* 67
Explanation: Adding 4 to each of the first two numbers gives the next two digits in a group of four; hence (2 + 4 = 6 and 3 + 4 = 7) = **67**

Q29. *Answer:* 78
Explanation: Alternate numbers rule applies to the second two numbers in the groups of four: 67 + 11 = 78 and 45 + 11 = 56

Q30. *Answer:* 27
Explanation: Alternate number rule applies to the second two numbers in the groups of four: 18 + 3 = 21 + 3 = 24 + 3 = **27**

Also available from Kogan Page

The Advanced Numeracy Test Workbook, Mike Bryon, 2003

Aptitude, Personality and Motivation Tests: Assess Your Potential and Plan Your Career, 2nd edition, Jim Barrett, 2004

The Aptitude Test Workbook, Jim Barrett, 2003

How to Master Personality Questionnaires, 2nd edition, Mark Parkinson, 2000

How to Master Psychometric Tests, 3rd edition, Mark Parkinson, 2004

How to Pass Advanced Aptitude Tests, Jim Barrett, 2002

How to Pass the Civil Service Qualifying Tests, 2nd edition, Mike Bryon, 2003

How to Pass Computer Selection Tests, Sanjay Modha, 1994

How to Pass Firefighter Recruitment Tests, Mike Bryon, 2004

How to Pass Graduate Psychometric Tests, 2nd edition, Mike Bryon, 2001

How to Pass the New Police Selection System, 2nd edition, Harry Tolley, Billy Hodge and Catherine Tolley, 2004

How to Pass Numerical Reasoning Tests, Heidi Smith, 2003

How to Pass Professional Level Psychometric Tests, 2nd edition, Sam Al-Jajjoka, 2004

How to Pass Selection Tests, 3rd edition, Mike Bryon and Sanjay Modha, 2005

How to Pass Technical Selection Tests, 2nd edition, Mike Bryon and Sanjay Modha, 2005

How to Pass Verbal Reasoning Tests, 3rd edition, Harry Tolley and Ken Thomas, 2006

How to Succeed at an Assessment Centre, 2nd edition, Harry Tolley and Robert Wood, 2005

IQ and Psychometric Test Workbook, Philip Carter, 2005

Test Your Own Aptitude, 3rd edition, Jim Barrett and Geoff Williams, 2003

For details on these titles and many more, or to order online, visit Kogan Page on the web at **www.kogan-page.co.uk**